Object Lessons for Church Groups

Vera Hutchcroft

BAKER BOOK HOUSE
Grand Rapids, Michigan

Copyright 1975
by Baker Book House Company

ISBN: 0-8010-4107-4

Second printing, November 1975

PHOTOLITHOPRINTED BY CUSHING - MALLOY, INC.
ANN ARBOR, MICHIGAN, UNITED STATES OF AMERICA
1975

To my youngest daughter,
Melonie,
who has been my critic
(and a good one),
a source of ideas,
and my 'guinea pig'
along with
the other young people
of our church.

Most of the songs or choruses suggested in this book can be found in *Sing Out,* 401 choruses for youth and adults, by Youth Ventures, Vancouver, British Columbia, Canada, 1972 and 1973.

Contents

1	What a Gift!	7
2	Hammer Versus Heat	11
3	Robes, Old and New	13
4	The Best Key	16
5	Fullness and Famine	19
6	The Best Pill	23
7	Pack Rats	27
8	What's Your Temperature?	31
9	Two Humans	35
10	Beautiful Feet	38
11	A Reminder of Christ	41
12	Cheer Up: God Loves the Worm and the Donkey	44
13	Happy Journey	49
14	Phony or Genuine	53
15	Danger, Keep Out!	57
16	Are You Running on Empty?	61
17	Three Cheers	64
18	Don't Be an Octopus	69
19	A Good Old Soul or a Miserable Heel	74
20	This Great Body	78
21	I Have a Bone to Pick with You	81
22	Be My Valentine	85
23	Sweet Repose	90
24	A Bottle of Medicine	93

1
What a Gift!

Objects

An apple core, a banana skin, some orange peelings, in a gift-wrapped box.

Purpose

To remind young people that God deserves first place in our lives.

Suggested Songs

Give of Your Best to the Master; I Surrender All; I Want to Do My Best for Jesus; All for Jesus.

Preparation

This is a two-part skit, given by two girls and one boy.

Gift wrap your "objects." You will also need a necklace, gift wrapped.

For the skit choose a girl and boy, about the same age, and an older girl.

You need not have an elaborate background. A chair or two on stage is sufficient.

Scene One

The skit opens with Barbara and Jean, her Sunday school teacher, meeting in the center of the stage. Jean has a beautifully wrapped gift in her hand.

Jean: (smiling) Hi, Barb, you're just the person I'm looking for. Happy Birthday. Here's something for you. I hope you like it. (She hands the gift to Barbara.)

Barbara: (excitedly) Hey, thanks! May I open it now? You always seem to know just what I want.

Jean: Sure, go ahead.

Barbara drops down on a chair and proceeds to open the package very excitedly. When she finally gets it open, her

7

eyes get big and her mouth drops open as if she can't believe what she is seeing. Finally, though, she begins to giggle.

Barbara: (shaking her head) For a dignified Sunday school teacher, you do the craziest things! What a joke! Imagine, (laughing) an apple core (picks up each one as she names them), a banana skin, and some orange peelings. Couldn't you find anything else in your garbage can to add to it? There is still room in the box. (Giggles again.)

Jean: I'm glad you like it.

Barbara: (still smiling, but not broadly) Oh, I love it, I love it! Now, where is my real birthday gift?

Jean: You've got it.

Barbara: (getting up, now thoroughly angry) I never—! And I thought you were my friend as well as my teacher! Well, no more! Here, you can have it back. (Grabs a handful of the peelings and throws them at Jean's feet. Then Barbara throws the box on the floor and stamps off as Jean walks away in the opposite direction, a determined but compassionate look on her face.)

Jean: (looking upward, says softly) Oh, Father, I hope this works.

(Clean up the peelings in preparation for the next scene.)

Scene Two

Barbara is seated by herself on the floor looking very unhappy. Mike, Jean's brother, comes strolling by in a rather happy-go-lucky way. As he sees Barbara, he walks over to her and stops by her side.

Mike: Well, well, how's my big sister's good friend and pupil?

Barbara: (keeps her head down, chin leaning on her hand and answers angrily) You've got your *adjectives* wrong! Change that good to worst!

Mike: I'll have to admit that **is** a switch. (Squats down beside her.) What happened between you and my sweet sister?

Barbara: (still angrily) Your adjectives are *still* wrong. Change that sweet to—to—*horrible, detestable, unbearable,* and *hateful.*

Mike: Hey, wait! I'm her little brother and *I* don't think

she's **that bad.** And besides, that still doesn't tell me what happened to bring on all this.

Barbara: (sneeringly) Your *dear* sister gave me a birthday present.

Mike: (raises his eyebrows) And *that's* supposed to be so awful? It's your birthday, isn't it?

Barbara: Yes. But do you know what the present was?

Mike: No, but she usually gives pretty good gifts. She gave me a neat camera my last birthday. Why?

Barbara: She emptied part of your garbage can in a box and wrapped it up!

Mike: (laughing heartily) That's a good one!

Barbara: (stands up, puts her hands on her hips and angrily says) Yeah, it's real funny!

Mike: (sobers down) Sorry, but that just doesn't sound like my big sister unless she meant it for a joke.

Barbara: I thought it *was* a joke at first but then she very seriously declared that it was for real.

Mike: (shakes his head) Come on; there is only one way to straighten out this situation. We'll find her and ask her.

Barbara: (hanging back) Oh, no, **we** don't. You, maybe, but not me. I've had enough!—of both her *and* her Sunday school class.

Mike: Says who? Come on.

(Mike grabs her arm and very reluctantly Barbara follows. As Mike and Barbara cross to the other side of the room, Jean starts coming toward them from the other side.)

Jean: (smiling) Hi, Mike and Barb.

Mike: You're just the one we're looking for, Sis. What's this about that kookie gift you gave Barb?

Jean. What do you mean?

Mike: Ah, come off it! You know what I mean. Why did you give Barb such a stupid present?

Jean: What's so stupid about an orange, a banana, and an apple?

Barbara: (sarcastically) You forgot to add peelings, dearie.

Excuse *me!* I'm wasting my time. (She turns and starts to leave but Mike grabs her arm.)

Mike: Oh, no, you don't! We're getting this settled. This doesn't sound like you, Jean. You'd better explain.

Jean: (pauses for a moment and then says) I will. Barb, you say you're a Christian. But lately you have been absent from church many times. And when I call you up or come over to ask you why you've missed, you've given excuses—you have a dress to shorten and get ready for your date the next day, you got in too late from your date the night before so you had to sleep in, or you had to wash and set your hair. When I've asked you to use that beautiful voice God has given you to sing to those lying ill in the nursing home, you're always too busy. Remember, when I asked you about it, you said you will have plenty of time to go to church and sing to sick people when you are older. In other words, you want to give what is left of your life to God after you've used up the best for yourself and Satan. You're going to give Him the core or the peelings of your life.

Barbara: (looks shocked and puts her hands over her face for a moment and then looks up over the top of her hands as she soberly says) You're right, Jean. The best Friend I have, and I'm giving Him my worst. Thank you, Jean, you've made your point. I think I'll dry that birthday present and keep it—if you'll come back and help me find it so I can pick it up. It will be a good reminder.

Jean (smiles) Gladly. But here, (puts her hand in her pocket and pulls out a small box) let me give you another birthday present first.

Barbara: Oh, Jean, thanks! (She pulls off the ribbon, opens the box, and brings out a necklace.) Oh, I love it! Thanks, again. But (sobers down), I think the first one is still the most valuable.

2
Hammer Versus Heat

Objects

A hammer, two pieces of plastic, and either a hot iron or some matches. (A hot iron works best.) If you use an iron, have on hand a piece of paper to lay on top of the plastic when you iron the two pieces together.

Purpose

To demonstrate that we influence others and make friends by showing love rather than by force.

Suggested Songs

Thy Loving Kindness; Lord, Lay Some Soul upon My Heart; I Want God's Way to Be My Way.

Preparation

Practice ironing the plastic together before you give this talk.

Presentation

I have here two pieces of plastic, a hammer, and an iron (or matches). The two pieces of plastic represent two young men. I'd like to join them—to make them loyal friends. So first we'll try force. (Lay one piece of plastic on top of the other and try to join them by pounding together.) As you can see, this isn't going to work. I could pound as long as I wanted to and then get angry and pound until I'm exhausted, but the only thing that would happen is that I'd finally smash them.

Have you ever tried making friends by force? If someone came up to you and said, "OK, you've got to be my friend or I'll beat you up," would you snap your fingers and be his friend? If you did, I'm sure you would be his friend because you felt he was someone worth having for a friend, not because he ordered you to.

It's the same way with other things we are asked to do. We

are more willing to do what we're asked if we aren't ordered or forced to do them.

Harshness does not unite people together. The Bible says, "A hot-tempered man starts fights and gets into all kinds of trouble" (Prov. 29:22, Living Bible). It also says, "An evil man sows strife; gossip separates the best of friends" (Prov. 16:28, Living Bible).

Wise Solomon knew that fists, swords, and harsh and unkind words will never make friends, or draw us closer together, or make others loyal to us. He calls those unkind words "cutting remarks" (Prov. 12:18, Living Bible) and that is just what those words do, they cut or separate friendships.

What will make us come together as friends? Let's go back to the plastic pieces. The hammer couldn't join them, but something else will and that something is heat. It will melt them together. (Join the plastic using either the iron or the matches.)

In the same way, the warmth of love will draw people together. How did God make you want to belong to Him? I'm sure it wasn't because He forced you. No, you were so convinced that He loved you so very much, you were glad to join His family. The Bible says, "The Lord hath appeared of old unto me, saying, Yea, I have loved thee with an everlasting love: therefore with lovingkindness have I drawn thee" (Jer. 31:3).

This warmth of love will even go farther. It will influence others to want to please the one who shows that love. When we realize how much Jesus loves us, we not only want to do what He asks us to do, but we also try to think of ways to do extra things to please Him. Love works the same way between people. As we show love to each other, we will live in harmony because we will be thinking of what will please the other person.

How do we show this love? Once again, let us go to the book that has all the answers. (Read I Cor. 13:4-7, Living Bible.)

Don't use harshness or force to try to gain loyal friends, use the warmth of love. It really works.

3
Robes, Old and New

Objects
Old, ragged, soiled, and torn clothes for the speaker to dress in. Four patches of various sizes and colors, and a supply of pins. Have ready also a good clean sheet.

Bible Story
Story taken from Matthew 22:2-13.

Purpose
To show that our goodness is not good enough to get us to heaven. Jesus is the only way.

Suggested Songs
Something Happened; He Saves, He Keeps; Yes, He Did; Stop and Let Me Tell You; Christ Is the Answer.

Preparation
Dress in the old clothes. If you don't have them, put on an old sheet which is soiled and full of holes.

Presentation
(Tell the story of Matt. 22:2-13.) When Jesus was here on earth He used stories to explain many things about heaven and how to get there. One story, called a parable, was about a king who prepared a great wedding feast for his son. The king sent out his servants and told them to say to those who had been invited, "Come to the wedding now for everything is ready." But those who were invited turned down the invitation. "Oh," they said, "we have too much to do; we're just not interested. Anyway, who wants to come?" Some even went so far as to hurt or kill the king's servants.

You can imagine how angry the king was. He gave orders to his soldiers, "Go out there and destroy those who have killed my servants."

Then he spoke to other servants and said, "The wedding feast is ready and we must have guests. The people I invited weren't worthy to come. So go out into the streets and invite anyone you see; the poor, the weak, and bad, and the good. Tell them all to come."

The servants did as the king told them and the wedding guests began to gather.

In those days the host supplied everyone with a special garment to wear at the wedding. But one man must have thought his clothes were just as good, if not better, than the wedding robe, so he didn't put the robe on.

When the king looked over the guests, he immediately saw the man who wasn't wearing the wedding robe, and he went to the man and asked, "My friend, why aren't you wearing the wedding garment?"

The man just looked at the king; there wasn't a thing he could say; he had no excuse.

So the king called to his servants and said, "Throw this man out. He is not worthy to come to my son's wedding."

What a terrible thing to happen! Do you know that there are people doing that same thing today? Such people want to go to heaven but they want to go their own way. Instead of asking Jesus into their lives and letting Him give them His robe of goodness, they want to be good their own way. But the Bible says that our righteousness or goodness is as filthy rags (Isa. 64:6). Not very nice, is it?

Still people admire Jesus; He is such a wonderful person. So they try to be like Him. They try to cover up some of the bad things they do with good things. Jesus said that was like putting a "piece of new cloth on an old garment" (Mark 2:21). Today we'd call that patching.

Let's do some pretending and see what some of these patches might be. Let's say Bob Patterson decides he's going to be better from now on, he's really going to make something of his life by copying that great—well, I suppose he'd call Him, teacher—Jesus. He'd say, "I really admire the way Jesus loves everyone. So now I'm going to love everyone, even that boy who gets on my nerves. (Pin one patch over a hole.) And Jesus was honest so I'm not going to cheat on any more tests. (Pin another patch over a hole.) Jesus was kind, too, so I'll be kind to my little brother from now on. (Pin another patch over a hole.) And Jesus was obedient to His parents so I will too. (Another patch.)

What is wrong with all this? First, the old robe of our goodness is still there. And what happens to all those good resolutions?

Bob says he is going to love everyone, but someone sticks out his foot and almost trips him. Bob suddenly forgets to love the person and swings at him with his fist. (Make a hole in the cloth.) He says he's going to be honest. But when the teacher offers a prize for the highest grade in spelling, he writes one word that he always has trouble with down on the edge of his shirt. (Make another hole.) He says he's going to be kind. But his book is too interesting to lay down just to play with his little brother. (Another hole.) As for being obedient to his parents, that's fine except when he thinks he can get by without being obedient. (Another hole.)

What has happened? That old robe of his own goodness isn't good enough, he's not strong enough in himself to do right.

What we do need is to ask Christ to come into our lives. Then He will get rid of that old robe of our goodness which really isn't any good, and give us His robe of goodness. (Take off the old robe and put on the new.) Along with this robe of His righteousness, Jesus gives us the power to do good and to be like Him. And someday He'll take us, still wearing His robe, to His home in heaven.

4

The Best Key

Objects

Several keys and a large sheet of paper on which is written two problems; (1) 1-3-6-10-?, (2) 1-1-2-3-5-8-? (Answers: no. 1—15, no. 2—13).

Purpose

To encourage young people to pray.

Suggested Songs

I Believe God; God Answers Prayer; God Can Do Anything but Fail; He Is Able; Why Worry when You Can Pray.

Presentation

Today we are going to talk about keys. Keys are very useful things. First, we can use them to lock things away, things such as a diary or secret love letters, or you might want to put your home work away from someone who wants to borrow it. Keys are also good for locking something in place, such as handcuffs you'd like to use on some children you baby sit. Keys are good for locking yourself in and everyone else out. Locked doors make us feel much braver when we're staying by ourselves on a dark stormy night. The key also unlocks doors which allow us to enter either bodily or with parts of the body, such as our hands. Keys unlock places such as a drawer where a box of candy has been stowed away.

There is another kind of key, (show them the puzzles written on paper a key which will solve a puzzle. Can you solve these two puzzles?

Using this as a background, let's think about another key, a spiritual key, one which unlocks the doors of spiritual growth and accomplishments. That key is prayer.

Prayer is the key which opens many doors. The most important door is the door to salvation. Romans 10:13 says, "For whosoever shall call upon the name of the Lord shall be saved." Saved from what? Saved *from* a life of unhappiness, unrest, insecurity, and eternal destruction, and saved *to* a life of joy, peace, and eternal life.

Prayer is also the key which opens the door to God's storeroom of supplies for our physical needs. The Bible says, "Let us therefore come boldly unto the throne of grace, that we may obtain mercy, and find grace to help in time of need" (Heb. 4:16). Luke 12 tells us how willing God is to supply us with food and clothing. That doesn't mean I can sit by idly and wait for God to drop a deluxe cheeseburger in my lap or slip a new pair of shoes on my feet. He expects me to do my part and then when I've done all I can, He'll do the rest. There is no excuse for laziness.

Another need we have is wisdom, and prayer unlocks this door too. James 1:5 says, "If any of you lack wisdom, let him ask of God, that giveth to all men liberally, and upbraideth not; and it shall be given him." Since He knows all the answers, He certainly is the best source of wisdom and knowledge. Once again, though, that doesn't mean He's going to flash the date of the beginning of World War I on a private screen in your mind if you haven't applied yourself to some old-fashioned digging into that detestable history book. (No, it's not *really* detestable, you just think so.)

God has the help for us if we just use the key when we have a time of trouble. Psalm 91:15 says, "He shall call upon me, and I will answer him; I will be with him in trouble; I will deliver him, and honour him." So if you're lost in the corridors of that new city school or you feel someone is following you as you walk home, use that key of prayer. God is there to answer.

There is another time when you need that key and that is when you need to escape from the tempter, Satan. Luke 21:36 says, "Watch ye therefore, and pray always, that ye may be accounted worthy to escape all these things that shall come to pass, and to stand before the Son of man." Jesus was tempted in all ways such as we are so He knows what we go through and will make a way of escape for us, as it says in I Corinthians 10:13.

Still another time we need this key is when we're in a puzzling situation and don't know what to do. God has the answer and will show it to us as we use this key of prayer. Jeremiah 33:3 says, "Call unto me, and I will answer thee, and shew thee great and mighty things, which thou knowest not." And Ephesians 3:20 says, "Now unto him that is able to do exceeding abundantly above all that we ask or think according to the power that worketh in us." We don't know the answers but God does and He promises to help us.

As the verse in Ephesians said, sometimes that key unlocks things which surprise us. Sometimes we are surprised to get more than we expected. But then there are also times when we ask for something and God says, "No, that isn't in My will."

One warning, though. There is a time when the key will not work. That is when the rust of sin corrodes it. Psalm 66:18 says, "If I regard iniquity in my heart, the Lord will not hear me." To "regard" here means to hang on to sins, refusing to ask for forgiveness for them. So the first thing that must be done is to ask God to forgive us and to cleanse our hearts from sin. That is one prayer He will always answer if we really mean it.

The Bible says, "Pray without ceasing" (I Thess. 5:17). So use that key continually; you'll never wear it out.

5

Fullness and Famine

Objects

A cup with a leak in it; filled with water at the beginning of the third part. Have a container handy to catch the drips.

Scripture Reference

Luke 15:11-24, 32.

Purpose

To compare what Satan offers and what he actually gives. To also show God's loving mercy.

Suggested Songs

Just as I Am; Lord, I'm Coming Home; Isn't He Wonderful; Can You Wonder; I Am Determined.

Preparation

Two people can give this talk—one can tell the Bible story and the other can make the application.

Presentation

A Story About Leaving

The Bible tells of a father who announced he was going to divide his property and all he had between his two sons. Such was the custom in those days—not waiting until one died to present the heirs with his wealth.

On hearing this, the youngest son decided that he wanted his in instant cash. He was discontented, and tired of home and father. Furthermore, he didn't really care what his father thought or felt. He was dreaming only of the gay time he thought was awaiting him if he could get away from home. Things out in the world looked so much more interesting and desirable.

Application: The same thing is happening today, in both

the natural and spiritual areas. But let's zero in on the spiritual area.

Many people are leaving their Heavenly Father and His protection today. However, it isn't a sudden move, a sudden decision or a change of mind. There are gradual steps that lead to this decision.

a. Carelessness is one. Such people begin to skip prayer time and reading God's Word. They also begin to drop out of regular attendance in church. They no longer want to spend time with the Heavenly Father, communing with Him.

b. Thoughtlessness is another step. Such people no longer care what their Heavenly Father wants. They would rather please others. They want to be thought of as a good guy or gal. They begin to arrange their lives the way they want it, not asking the will of God.

c. Getting their eyes on the world and what it has to offer is another step. What Satan has to offer begins to look good and he makes sure it does look bright and promising. Wrong begins when we do *look* and consider. Since we no longer care what the Father wants and our love for Him has begun to cool, we compare Satan's offerings with the Father's in the light of what we want and what will gratify the flesh.

A Story About Fullness

The youngest son now felt he had it made. He had everything he wanted: money and the good life that went with it. At any rate, he thought it was good. He went a long way from home and proceeded to spend this money. The Bible says he "wasted his substance [or money] with riotous living" (v. 13). Can't you imagine what he did? He bought beautiful and expensive garments and robes, stayed in the most exclusive inns, ate and drank the richest food and wine. He gathered around himself a great circle of friends, both men and women, wining and dining them, and no doubt presenting them with costly gifts. And they, in turn, heaped on him flattery and praise. Oh, he was the most! Oh, yes! to the younger son, this was *the* life.

Application: Satan makes everything seem so glittering and wonderful. He appeals to the senses. He says, "You take this dope, or drink this beer or wine and you'll forget all the problems you've been having." Or "Go with this crowd, you'll be popular, one of the gang." Or "Why not free love? You're only young once. Enjoy the human passions." Or, "Just do what *you* want for once and have fun." And for a time he seems to be right; life seems to be great.

A Story About Emptiness

Yes, the youngest son was really enjoying himself. His cup seemed to be full and overflowing with the best and most enjoyable things in life. (Fill the leaky cup with water and hold it so that the drips will show while you complete the next part of the story.) But then what happened? His bag of money became lighter and one day he found himself without any money. Not only that, but there was a famine in the land so he couldn't even find a good job. And to top it all off, those friends who called him a jolly good fellow, now as if by common consent, disappeared. From an abundance, he came now to complete emptiness. He had to take the only job he could find—a pig-keeper, one of the most degrading occupations of the day.

Application: This is a good picture of those who serve Satan. He promises so much and seems to have so much to offer us. But he never shows us the end result until it is too late. He doesn't show the ruined health that comes after one is bound by the habit of drink. He doesn't show the unhappiness and tears and emptiness which is the end product of the life given to Satan.

A Story About Home, Sweet Home

I'm glad the picture isn't hopeless. The youngest son finally "wised up." He looked at himself in his rags and filth and wondered what he was doing in the pig pen. He decided he'd go home and, as he was no longer worthy to be a son, he'd be just a hired servant. But the father who had been waiting and longing for his son not only permitted him to come back, but actually ran to welcome him back as the long lost son that he was. The father gave a large welcoming feast.

Application: When we realize our mistake in serving Satan rather than our heavenly Father, we too have a way back to Him. He longs for us. If we make the first step toward Him, He will meet us more than half way. Such a loving, forgiving heavenly Father we have who says, "If we confess our sins, he is faithful and just to forgive us our sins, and to cleanse us from all unrighteousness" (I John 1:9).

6

The Best Pill

Objects
Bottles of pills of different colors and sizes

Purpose
To show that the "gos-pill" gives promise of health, happiness, and hope for the future—far more than any manufactured pill.

Suggested Songs
Tell Me the Old Old Story; Christ Is the Answer; If Jesus Said It; There's Power in the Blood.

Preparation
Gather many types of pills and put them on display. *CAUTION!*—Keep a *very* close watch on the pills to make sure no one takes any of them.

Presentation
Today we are going to speak about pills. (Show the display.) There are big pills and little pills; white pills, green pills, yellow pills (mention especially the colors you have). There are flat pills, long pills, and three-cornered pills. There are strong pills and weak pills, pills for children and adults. Pills for headaches, colds, pains, nausea, and the blues. Most pills have their place and are good for something.

The best pill of all, though, is the one we're going to talk about now, the "gos-pill." I know that sounds way out but it isn't quite as foolish as it sounds. Let's make some comparisons and you'll see what I mean.

1. Pills are for people who need them, whether they are rich or poor, young or old, no matter what their race.

The "gos-pill" is also for everyone who needs it—and *everyone* needs it. It was given to the rich young ruler; and Matthew

11:5 tells about the gospel being preached to the poor. Romans 1:16 tells us that the gospel is for both Jew and Greek.

2. Pills are a mystery to most of us. We don't understand how they work, but we have faith that the doctor and the maker of the pills know what they are talking about. So we just swallow them.

Paul, in Colossians 1:26, 27, speaks about the mystery of the gospel. We don't understand how that God's Son, alive before the foundation of the world, could come into this world as a baby, live a sinless life, and finally lay down His life on the cross, and rise again on the third day. We don't understand how believing on this Person can rid us of our sins, give us power to live above sin, and give us a sure hope of heaven after this life. No, we can't understand it, but through faith we know it is true. We can say along with Paul, "I know whom I have believed, and am persuaded that he is able to keep that which I have committed unto him against that day" (II Tim. 1:12).

3. Sometimes the pills are hard to swallow. Some people can take pills easier than others.

Some people are able to accept the "gos-pill" much easier than others, too. Some seem to accept it on faith the minute they hear about it, while others must be persuaded for quite some time, and hesitate as they think things over. They wonder if the end result justifies the acceptance of the gospel.

4. If you have faith in the pills and take them, they will give the results they are supposed to give. If you don't take the pills, you might not recover.

Mark 16:15 talks about the preaching of the gospel and then goes on to say, "He that believeth and is baptized shall be saved." In other words, if we believe on this "gos-pill" and follow directions, it will do the work it claims to do. Romans 1:16 says, "The gospel of Christ is the power of God unto salvation to every one that believeth." Mark 16:15 goes on to say, "He that believeth not shall be damned."

5. If you are sick and the doctor prescribes a pill, and you take that pill, you can expect to see signs that the pill

is working. You may feel the results immediately, but often you may have to wait a few hours.

The Bible tells us that the acceptance of the "gos-pill" will be followed by outward signs because of something done inside, in the heart. II Corinthians 5:17 says "Therefore if any man be in Christ, he is a new creature: old things are passed away; behold, all things are become new." Just before Christ went up into heaven, He said this: (Read Mark 16:17, 18).

6. To a sick person, pills give hope of better days ahead. Some pills even take the user on a trip, though many times a bad one.

The accepter of the "gos-pill" also has hope of a more wonderful life. David knew about this when he said, "Thou wilt shew me the path of life: in thy presence is fulness of joy; at thy right hand there are pleasures for evermore" (Ps. 16:11). And for those who accept the "gos-pill" there is going to be the greatest trip of all, the trip to heaven. The Bible says, "We give thanks to God and the Father of our Lord Jesus Christ, for the hope which is laid up for you in heaven, whereof ye heard before in the word of the truth of the gospel" (Col. 1:3a, 5). No bad trip there, all glorious and wonderful!

7. Pills are extensively advertised, especially in medical circles. Then, as the user of the pills finds relief, he is anxious to tell others, "Hey, I took Bentley's Cure-all and now look, no more spots on my face. Won't Griselda think I'm the *most!*"

God expects us to advertise the "gos-pill" too. Jesus said in Mark 16:15, "Go ye into all the world, and preach the gospel to every creature."

"Oh," you are saying, "but I'm going to be a secretary, not a preacher."

We don't have to be a preacher to advertise this gospel. If you have accepted this "gos-pill" and it has done great things for you, go and tell others about it—advertise it.

8. Pills are usually very expensive.

The "gos-pill" cost more than any other pill. It cost God His Son, and it cost Jesus His life on the cross. He offers it freely to us, though. We can be so thankful that He does, for none of us would have enough riches to buy such a wonderful "pill."

9. Not everyone will believe that your pills are the best. In fact, some may disagree rather violently.

Even Paul, as he preached from place to place, found that not everyone would accept the gospel of Jesus Christ. Paul was beaten many times and thrown in jail. The people of that time had done even worse to Jesus, so Paul wasn't reluctant to suffer for his Savior. Paul said to Timothy, "Be thou partaker of the afflictions of the gospel according to the power of God" (II Tim. 1:8b). Paul also said, "I am not ashamed of the gospel of Christ" (Rom. 1:16a). I hope you're not ashamed of this wonderful "gos-pill" either.

Accept this most wonderful of all pills—the "gos-pill." There is an eternal guarantee with it.

7

Pack Rats

Object
A pet rat if available; otherwise a picture of a rat.

Purpose
To encourage youth to weigh the things that look so inviting to see if they are worthwhile in the light of God's Word.

Suggested Songs
I Want God's Way to Be My Way; I Am Determined; Stand Fast (Gal. 5:1, 13, 22, 23); Follow, I Will Follow Thee.

Presentation
Today we have one of God's creatures that most people, especially ladies, don't like. Actually, there are good reasons not to like them—if they are not a pet. They are very destructive, and carry diseases. They also reproduce very fast and can soon take over, or infect, a large area.

There are many kinds of rats and many relatives in the rodent family but the one I want to mention today is the pack rat. It is also called the wood rat because it lives in the woods and desert areas of North America. Some pack rats build huge homes from sticks and brush. They get the name of pack rat, however, because they collect bright objects such as buttons, pieces of glass, or bottle tops. They don't assess the object to see if it has any real value or usefulness to them; if it is bright and shining, it is desirable.

Satan is trying to make pack rats out of us. He holds out things that look bright and glittering and he hopes we'll grab them. He wants us to think that we must have such things. He tries to cloud our minds to keep us from assessing the real value of things. The Bible says Satan is transformed into an angel of light (II Cor. 11:14) trying to make bad look good.

Paul tells us to "Prove all things," and then, "hold fast that which is good" (I Thess. 5:21).

How are we to know which is the good and which is the bad? First, we can see if they will pass the Philippians 4:8 test. (Read both the King James and the Living Bible translations.) Will our thoughts be as this verse says if we cling to this certain way or action? Secondly, we can assess what will be the outcome. Jesus said, "Wherefore by their fruits ye shall know them" (Matt. 7:20). I know He is talking about false prophets but this is also a good rule for other things. Look at a few glittering things Satan may try to tempt us with and weigh them against Philippians 4:8 and Matthew 7:20.

1. *Popularity at any price.* There is nothing wrong with being popular with the right crowd and being liked and respected by everyone—if you don't have to sacrifice your Christian principles to do so. But if you have to help someone cheat on a test, join in with the crowd's dirty stories, or go to places where you know a follower of Jesus Christ should never be, then the price is too high. The fruit will be a guilty conscience, a Christian light that is all but extinguished, and the fact that you have grieved Jesus.

2. *Getting grades the easy way.* It may look great to skip the studying and then copy from someone else's paper but that is dishonest and contrary to Philippians 4:8, and the fruit is stupidity.

3. *Getting away from parents and their supervision.* Of course, I'm talking about those who are teen-agers. Everyone must leave their parents some time, but until they are of age, God has given children parents for a very good reason. Satan may make running away look wonderful but the world is a cold, cold place for someone who has no place to go. Besides disobeying Christ who tells us to obey and honor our parents, the fruits too often are a bad record with the law officials, loss of purity and health, and unhappiness for both you and your parents.

4. *That gorgeous hunk of man,* (or that cute chick), unsaved, but who, nevertheless, you must have as your boyfriend or

girl friend. This is one of Satan's most glittering temptations. But the Bible tells us not to be unequally yoked together with an unbeliever (II Cor. 6:14).

"Oh," but the cry comes, "who's talking about being yoked or joined together?"

Dating that certain person always precedes marriage. And even if you don't marry that guy or gal, they are sure to draw you farther away from God, not toward Him. You have different masters, different ideals, and different goals—at least you should have. The fruits of such companionship are all wrong.

5. *Smoking, drinking, and drugs.* Satan has a way of making young people think they should at least try some of these things. "After all," he says, "who wants to be thought of as a chicken or a square?" He encourages the advertisements which picture these people as those who are blooming in health and happiness. He doesn't want you to see the true picture—the cancerous body, the staggering drunkard, or the blown mind. Once again, the fruit is not right.

6. *Free love.* What a very false expression—a lie from Satan to make it seem more desirable. Nothing is really free and this type of love is most expensive. Satan says, "You're only human; satisfy your inward craving and get a thrill. You needn't be shackled by marriage or promises of any kind." A wise God knows better, however, and has your best happiness at heart when he lays down rules to govern your life. He knows the emotional involvement that leaves a scar, the unwanted baby, the diseases, and the guilt. The fruit of "free" love makes it very expensive.

7. *False religions.* In recent years there has been the great movement of "The Jesus people." Young people flocked to these gatherings and became involved with following Jesus. Some, though, joined only because it was the popular thing to do. Now these people are being attracted by Satan to false religions which look very glittering with their spectacular show of power. Too many of these false religions worship Satan and so the power comes from Satan. Yes, Satan does have power.

But remember, God is more powerful. John tells us to try the spirits (Read I John 4:1-4).

These are just a few of the things Satan holds up to us as glittering and therefore desirable and valuable. But let's not be like the pack rat and accept something just because it looks good. Instead, let's do as Paul advises: "Prove all things." And after we have proved what is good, let's "hold fast" to it.

8

What's Your Temperature?

Objects
Different kinds of thermometers.

Purpose
Love without works is no love. Help the young people to examine their hearts to see how great is their love for Jesus.

Suggested Songs
For God So Loved the World; Trust and Obey; I Love Him Better Every Day; I Have Decided to Follow Jesus.

Preparation
Involve the young people. Hand out the Bible references to the young people to be read as needed.

After the young people discuss the three problems suggested, be prepared to tell them what Jesus would have them do. You may have additional problems to bring up which relate specifically to your group.

Presentation
Today we have some thermometers. A thermometer is a gauge to measure cold and heat. If I want to fry some potatoes, I'd like to know if the fat or oil is hot enough to fry them without having them soak up unnecessary oil. I'd also like to know if the oil is getting too hot and will cook the potatoes too fast. On a cold morning, if my thermometer should say fifty degrees below zero, I'm not going outside in a bikini. My gauge tells me I'd better be wrapped like a cocoon or stay in the house by my fireplace.

The Bible tells us that we also have a gauge that determines the amount of love we have in our hearts for our Savior. That gauge is obedience.

These thermometers are easy to read and so are our actions

easy to read. If a husband asks his wife to iron his shirt and she refuses without a very good reason, he would have good reason to think her love for him was rather cool; especially if this happened continually. If a boy said, "I love you, mommy," but put his friends' wishes before his mother's, she would probably doubt if he loved her a great deal.

A little girl was asked to show the meaning of love. First, she ran to her teacher and gave her a resounding kiss. "That's fine," her teacher said, "Now can you show me another way to say you love me?" The little girl thought a minute and then proceeded to straighten up some books in the room.

The Bible has a good supply of verses on this subject so we need not doubt our Heavenly Father's will. Let's read a few of them. (Read, or have read, the following verses which have been handed out: John 14:15; I John 2:3; I John 2:15; I John 3:18; I John 4:8; I John 4:20, 21; I John 5:3; Matt. 6:24; I Samuel 15:22.)

All of these verses point to the fact that our actions show us the degree of love we possess for our God, and He would have our actions rather than ou rwords or religious motions say, "I love you."

Actions aren't the easiest way to say, "I love you, God." Some of God's commandments are just the opposite from what we'd like to do. These incidents might come up in your life. If you were the Christian person involved, how would you react as an obedient follower of Christ?

No. 1. Frank was running for school president against Pete. Besides being a Christian, Frank was near the top in grades and had real leadership qualities. Pete, however, was more popular with the kids, for he had a large allowance and spent it freely on his friends. To top it all off, he was a football star. When the votes were counted, Pete won. What should Frank's reaction be, knowing that he was better qualified for the office? Why? (After discussion, read I Cor. 13:4, 5, Living Bible.)

No. 2. Jane and Betty had been friends for quite some time, but lately Betty had been about the end! It was, "Jane, can I borrow fifty cents?" or "Jane, I knew you wouldn't mind, so I copied your algebra paper," and "I know I had promised to go to lunch with you, but I met Angie and just forgot." Or, "Your boy friend isn't so bad! I may just see if I can get a date with him."

Christian means to be Christ-like. How can Jane be like Christ in this set-up? (Remind students of I Cor. 13:4.)

No. 3. Gail thought she must be about the busiest girl this side of the Atlantic. She had home work (and grades didn't come easy with her), she did quite a bit of baby sitting, and she was a cheer leader which meant going to most of the school games. Because she was a Christian, she also went to church Sunday morning and evening and youth services on Thursday nights. In fact she was so busy, Saturday was about the only day she had to sleep in and do all the other things that needed to be done (and sometimes baby sitting took part of that time).

Lately her mother, who was not a Christian, was getting rather upset (to put it mildly) at her messy room and the number of times she begged off doing things, such as dishes, around the home. What should Gail do, and why? (Remind pupils of a child's duty to parents as commanded in the Bible.)

Why, do you think, did God make such a big thing out of obedience? Why didn't He just say, "Love me and then do as you please?" Perhaps you may think it was just to keep us under His thumb. But, actually, it was just the opposite; it was because of His love for us. He knows what is best for us and what is best for others. The whole principle of Christianity is love. God loved us and sent His Son. Jesus loved us and died. He draws us to Himself through love. Now He wants our love and He wants us to show that Christ-like love to others so they will accept Him too.

How much love does your love-gauge show you have for your Savior? If your thermometer shows that your love is rather cold, you can bring up the temperature by getting to know

God better. You can do that by talking to Him and reading His love letter, the Bible. To know Him is to love Him and to love Him is to obey Him.

9

Two Humans

Objects
A mother and father

Purpose
To foster better relationships in the family and help youth realize that their parents are human.

Preparation
Select as objects two parents who are liked and respected.

Presentation
Today we have two live objects; they are mom and dad (name). We're going to talk a little about family relationships.

The Bible gives two commands concerning parents which take in every part of our actions and attitudes toward them. The first is, "Children, obey your parents...." The other is, "Honor thy father and mother." The first is very easy to understand, but the second takes a bit more thought.

They are human. Let's take a good look at our two objects, now. The first thing I want you to notice about them is that they are, (and don't laugh) human. Queer as it may seem, that is something many young people seem to forget. What do we mean when we say they are human? For one thing, they have feelings. (Gently pinch the man and ask him if he felt it.) If I had pinched him very hard, he might have gotten angry and shouted, "Ouch," for he also has emotions. And this is where some difficulties begin. Teen-agers may not realize that mom and dad have off days, when they don't feel quite up to par. Maybe some bills are due and there isn't enough money to pay them, or perhaps they've received some bad news and haven't been able to sleep. Now, you'd think they would be able to keep cool and trust completely in God's wisdom so that nothing could upset them. Remember, I said they are human and human beings are not perfect. Accept your parents as they are—people who have feelings and emotions.

They have feelings; don't downgrade them. Besides having feelings on the outside, they also have feelings on the inside; they're sensitive. You can hurt their feelings, just like they can hurt yours. To be rude, sarcastic, and to make degrading remarks about them will make them feel sad, though they may try to hide it. To forget their birthday, to never notice when they do something especially nice hurts them—just like it would you.

Treat them like company. Think of someone you want to impress. How do you act? You talk politely, in a moderate tone. You don't butt in when he is talking. You smile and act interested when he is speaking. You say, "please," "thank you," "excuse me," "I'm sorry," at the proper times. In other words, you're putting forth your company manners.

Communicate. I want you to notice one more thing about this mom and dad; they have two ears and a mouth. That suggests communication; neither the talking or the listening should be one-sided. Since both parents and children are human, there are sure to be problems. Keep the lines of communication open so that children's as well as parents' problems can be discussed.

Some teens say that their parents won't listen to them. If you are in that situation, bring in a neutral party to help to be honest.

Be honest with them all the time. In fact, be honest all the time. You don't like to come home and find your parents gone without a note telling where they are. Well, they don't like to have you leave without knowing where you are going.

You are their responsibility. They brought you into the world, so you are their responsibility. When you are young, they have to admit you belong to them, no matter what your actions are (although sometimes they may hate to admit it). They know what they teach you will reflect later on how happy and successful you are. If your parents are Christians, when they get to heaven they will have to answer to God for the training they gave you. So with all this staring them in the face, don't be surprised if they get uptight when you don't follow instructions.

They want to please Jesus and make heaven their home. There is something this mom and dad have that you could never see. They have a spiritual nature—a soul. Their relationship with God is important, and very close, because they are a son and daughter of God.

As children of God they wish to please Him. In every part of their life they ask themselves, "What would He have me to do?" If you should ask permission to spend the weekend camping with a group of kids, your parents don't just ask if that would be nice for you, or, if they need you at home for something special. Rather, they ask if God would want them to give you permission. Will this outing be pleasing to God and draw you closer to the Lord? You see, for Christian parents serving Christ and raising their family is all mixed up together. How thankful you should be that it is.

Perhaps some of you are thinking: my parents are not Christians. God asks you even then to obey and honor them. Unknown to your parents, (and perhaps to you, too) God uses them very often to direct your steps and life in His way.

Pray for them. Because your parents are human, because you are their responsibilities, because they have a soul and will stand before God some day to give an account of their stewardship, pray for them. Ask God to give them wisdom, serenity of spirit through all the trials of life, and the joy of God each day.

10

Beautiful Feet

Object
A pair of bare feet (see preparation section)

Purpose
To remind the youth that God and other people notice when they are walking as God would have them.

Suggested Songs
Follow, I Will Follow Thee; I'll Go Where You Want Me to Go; Stand Up for Jesus; Onward Christian Soldiers; Just a Closer Walk with Thee; I Have Decided to Follow Jesus.

Preparation
Ask one of the pupils to sit on a chair with his bare feet resting on another chair or on a table in view of everyone. Bring also a few headlines of peaceful or hostile activities.

Presentation
Today we have a very simple object to talk about—yes, simple, but very beautiful. You don't agree? The Bible says feet are beautiful: once in Isaiah 52:7, and again in Romans 10:15. Let's read the one in Romans. (Read)

You'll have noticed the Bible didn't say *all* feet are beautiful, only the feet of those who preach the gospel of peace. Ever since feet were formed by God, they have been dashing about after peace, or trouble, or unrest. Eve, in the beginning of the Bible turned her feet toward Satan as she listened to the tempter. Today many people still turn their feet toward wrong, though a few walk in the way of peace. (Read the headlines you've brought.)

Why, do you suppose, did the Bible put the emphasis on feet rather than the mouth or hands? It must be because our feet take us, or begin the journey, to whatever activity we are going to engage in. Proverbs 6:13 actually talks about feet that speak.

Speaking Feet: How do our feet speak? In two ways: in the direction they are turned, and the fastness or slowness of their gait at specific times.

Watch a troublemaker and you will see his feet turn to run quickly toward any disturbance. Should a person of authority pass by—a police officer or the principal—many times his feet will turn and take him slowly slouching off in the other direction.

On the job your employer is probably sure your feet speak. Some feet, the ones that will probably get fired, are those which are slow to move when there is a job to be done, and fast to get around the corner and out of sight when they expect the boss to give them something to do. Contrary to that, though, are the feet which travel quickly to follow instructions; those which are around when there is extra work to be completed, even if it means extra steps and staying late. Those feet belong to the one who gets the raise and promotion.

In school, the feet which turn toward the disturbance to add to the trouble are noted by the teacher. The feet that stay in their place when the teacher is out of the room belong to those who are respected by others. The teacher can soon catalogue each pupil by the direction in which his feet go.

At home, your feet speak to your parents and tell them if you are to be trusted.

Yes, your feet are a testimony about the type of person you are. And that testimony is very important if you are a Christian. It influences others toward Christ or away from Him. If your feet are an active testimony of your love for Christ and His commandments, you can say that your feet are beautiful for they take you to bring the gospel of peace.

When you come right down to it, I'm not sure if these feet are beautiful, for they have been rather still during our lesson. But God knows. Let's hope they are and that all feet here today are beautiful. Do you know where all beautiful feet are going to walk someday? Right through the gates of heaven and onto those streets of gold.

11

A Reminder of Christ

Object
A Christmas tree

Purpose
To help youth see more of Christ in Christmas.

Suggested Songs
Sing Christmas carols.

Preparation
Decorate the tree in the usual way with lights and bright tinsel and balls. Put a star on top and gifts underneath.

Presentation
Christmas is almost a magic word bringing many pictures to our minds: lights, Christmas trees, gifts, and decorations. But I'm wondering how many times the true picture of Christmas, one that should be at the center of Christmas activities, flashes into our minds.

Today I want to use the Christmas tree as an object lesson, hoping that this symbol of Christmas will remind us of the One who was born on that first Christmas Day.

Almost all Christmas trees, unless they are artificial, are evergreen trees. As long as they are living these trees are green the year round. Other trees seem to sleep for a period of time, but not the evergreen.

How like our Savior this is. The Bible says He neither slumbers nor sleeps (read Ps. 121:1-4). How wonderful to know that our God, whether it be God the Father, God the Son, or God the Holy Spirit, is watching over us all hours of the day and night, and is right there listening when we call to Him.

We notice that the Christmas tree glitters. The balls, the ropes, and the tinsel are all made to sparkle, to catch the eye.

Isn't this also like Jesus? His physical features weren't so outstanding that they drew the people to Him while He was here on earth. It was rather His inward love shining out and manifesting itself in His actions, that drew people to Him. Jesus is in heaven now with His Father, but as our lives reflect His love, we attract others to love and serve Him.

Another thing we notice about almost every Christmas tree are the lights—lights of every color. Beautiful, aren't they?

How easy it is to see Jesus in the lights, for He says, "I am the light of the world: He that followeth me shall not walk in darkness, but shall have the light of life" (John 8:12).

What does light do? It shows the way to the place we wish to go. Where do you wish to go?—to a place of love, happiness, satisfaction, security? Jesus shows us the way. He beckons for us to come to Him and He will give us all these things plus heaven.

Under the tree we see gifts. Let's face it, we all like to get gifts, especially from those we love. And we like to give gifts. That is a mutual expression of our feelings for each other.

Giving and receiving gifts should remind us of the greatest gift ever given to man, the gift of God's Son. That was the supreme gift of love, as John 3:16 says (read that verse). In Romans 6:23 we read, "The gift of God is eternal life through Jesus Christ our Lord." There are costly gifts given and received each year but none as costly as that one given on the first Christmas when God gave His only Son. And this "Gift" in turn gave us an added gift some thirty-three years later as He gave His life on the cross.

On top of Christmas trees we often see a star. That reminds us of the star the wise men followed long ago. The wise men said, "Where is he that is born King of the Jews? for we have seen his star in the east, and are come to worship him" (Matt. 2:2). They were looking for a King of the Jews, but Jesus isn't a King of the Jews, He is King of Creation. It is one thing to ask Jesus to come into our life, but it is another to ask Him to rule that life. This means that we take second place. It won't be what do *I* want to do, but what will *You* have me to do. As you look at the many stars on the Christmas trees, I hope you will ask yourself if Jesus *really* is your King.

12

Cheer Up: God Loves the Worm and the Donkey

Objects

A worm and a donkey costume (see preparation section)

Purpose

To remind young people that God has a place for *everyone*. He's just as pleased with the deeds of the less talented as with those of the gifted. He wants us to faithfully do our best.

Suggested Songs

I Know the Lord Has Laid His Hand on Me; I Want to Do My Best!; If You Will Give What You Have.

Preparation

From a blanket make a costume to resemble a donkey. When it is finished, throw it over two boys who will crawl, one behind the other.

Pin a small towel, or cloth, on the back of the blanket for a tail. Make the head from the foot of a nylon stocking. From a large piece of cardboard cut a large T shape, rounding the edges to form ovals. The middle oval should be about as long as the foot of the nylon stocking. Put the middle oval in the nylon and stuff cloth on both sides of it and around it, bending the other two ovals outside the stocking to form ears. Gather the top part of the nylon around the base of the long ears and pin it to the front of the blanket. With marker pens, draw in eyes, mouth, and nostrils.

Presentation

Today I'd like to talk about two creatures in God's creation. The first is a worm. (Show the worm.) Few people like the worm. Worms are slimy, squishy, and wiggly. Actually our little humble worm is quite valuable. Besides tempting a fish to grab your hook, he is very good for the soil. However, when you say that you feel like a worm, you're not thinking of all these valuable things about a worm, but rather you're feeling low down, ashamed, and of no account. When you're feeling that way, remember God loves even the worm.

Let's talk about another animal. He is more difficult to bring in, so I've left him outside. Oh, he got in! (Have the two boys in the donkey costume come in, braying as they enter.)

Since our donkey has gotten in, we'll let him stay. (Have the boys sit on the floor with the costume still over them or let them take it off and sit down.)

Has anyone ever called you a donkey? When people call you a donkey, they aren't thinking of the long-eared friend, who kindly gives rides to little children. No, they probably mean that you are dumb and ridiculous. But God loves the donkey, just as He loves the worm. I know He does because He used both creatures to help Him teach lessons to some of His followers. Let's go back to the worm.

Worm No. 1: (Briefly tell the story of Exod. 16:1-31.) God used the worm to help Him teach a lesson in obedience when the children of Israel were journeying to the promised land. They had run out of food and were complaining to Moses (which actually was the same as complaining to God because God had chosen Moses to lead His people). Even though they complained rather than trusted, God sent food in the form of tiny wafers. This food rained from heaven every morning except on the Sabbath day. God's instructions to His people were to gather just as much food as they would need for each day, no more and no less, except for the sixth day when they were to gather enough food for two days. In spite of this wonderful miracle the people did not completely trust God. Some of them tried to keep some food for the next day. And this is where the worms came in. The worms got in the food and made it unfit to eat on the second day. Now just to show you that this was something special, when the food was kept over on the seventh day, God's day, it did not get wormy.

Worm No. 2: (Tell the story of Jonah.) Another time when God used a worm to teach a lesson was after Jonah refused to warn the people of Nineveh of God's anger and tried to run from God. You remember that Jonah finally landed in the stomach of a big fish. God was merciful and gave Jonah another chance. After the big fish vomited up Jonah, he gladly went and preached to the people of Nineveh who listened and repented.

Jonah didn't like that either. The people had been so wicked that Jonah thought they should still be destroyed. While Jonah was complaining, God caused a gourd plant to come up and shade Jonah from the sun. Then, and here is where our little worm comes in, "God prepared a worm when the morning rose the next day, and it smote the gourd that it withered" (Jonah 4:7). When the plant died, Jonah again became angry. God wanted to show Jonah that if he was so concerned about the destruction of the little plant, God was much more concerned about the destruction of thousands of people. And to teach Jonah this lesson, God used the little worm.

How did the worm fulfill God's purpose? By living the way it was made to live, in the place where God wanted it to live.

And here is a lesson for us. We may feel as useless and insignificant as a little worm, but if we yield ourselves to God in our everyday living, we will be as pleasing to God as those great ministers who preach to thousands of people.

Sermons are preached by our actions. We teach the lesson of kindness by helping others. We teach the lesson of purity by refusing to laugh at dirty stories. We teach the lesson of joy by being cheerful at all times. These are all simple things that each person can do in his own environment. This is serving God.

Donkey: (Tell the story of Numbers 22.) Let's go to our next humble animal, the donkey or, as the Bible calls him, the ass. He was used many times as a means of transportation, not quite in the class of a Cadillac, more like a Ford or Chevrolet.

During the time Moses was leading the children of Israel to the promised land God used a donkey to teach a lesson in faithfulness. The Israelites were in the land of Moab and the Moabites were very afraid and distrustful of the Israelites. So knowing where Balaam, a prophet of God lived, Balak the king of Moab, sent word to the prophet to come and curse the children of Israel. Balaam asked God's permission and God said, *"No,* don't curse the people for they're blessed by me."

After Balak learned that God wouldn't allow Balaam to curse the Israelites, he decided to try to tempt Balaam. He sent honorable men to try to impress Balaam with the message Balak would give Balaam a place of honor in the kingdom.

That offer sounded good to Balaam and he decided to talk to God once more to see if God had changed His mind. God said words to this effect: "Okay, if you care more for honor and money, go."

So Balaam got on his faithful ass and started on his way. But God wanted to impress on the prophet that he was displeasing God, so He sent an angel with a sword after Balaam. The trouble was, however, that Balaam didn't see the angel. His ass did. Instead of keeping to the path, she went out into a field. Balaam became very upset with the ass and he hit her.

The next section of the path went through a vineyard. There was a high wall on either side of the narrow path. An angel stood on the path, blocking the way. This time the ass pushed herself against the wall, hoping to get by. In doing so she crushed Balaam's foot. Once again Balaam hit the ass.

Finally they came to a place so narrow that there wasn't any hope of turning one way or the other. Once again an angel blocked the path. The ass decided this was it, and lay down. Balaam, now furious, beat the ass again.

And now the ass did something asses don't ordinarily do: she began to talk. "What have I done wrong," she asked, "that you've beat me these three times?"

"Because you're being disobedient and stubborn with me," Balaam replied. "If I had a sword in my hand I'd kill you."

"In all the years I've served you have I ever done anything like this?" the ass asked. And Balaam had to admit she hadn't.

Then God opened Balaam's eyes and he saw the angel with

the sword in his hand. Now it was Balaam's turn to be frightened and he fell to the ground. He had good reason to be afraid. The angel explained that if the ass hadn't stopped, the angel would have killed Balaam because Balaam's heart was far from the Lord. The angel said, "Now that you have started, go on with the trip but speak only the words which the Lord will give you to speak."

God used the dumb, humble ass to teach a lesson to the prophet. At first the ass only did what came naturally to her, but God also used her later to do something quite out of the ordinary, for who has heard a donkey carrying on a conversation? God had a job that needed to be done and He found an obedient creature, the ass, and used her.

Who knows what God has in store for you? You may feel yourself as humble and dumb as the worm and donkey. Maybe you don't have any outstanding talents. But God isn't looking for a person proud of his own talents, thinking only about himself and what he can get out of life. God is looking for a person filled with the love of God, ready to stay and do the ordinary humble task faithfully. Whether the task be ordinary or unusual, God will reward each for his faithfulness in whatever task assigned to him. All we have to do is to be faithful. And at last God will say, "Well done, thou good and faithful servant."

13
Happy Journey

Objects
A toy car which looks as if it has been in a wreck and/or a picture of a wrecked car.

Purpose
To point out what makes a successful or unsuccessful marriage.

Suggested Songs
In Times Like These; Like A Melody; Christ Is the Answer; Hallelujah, I'm Walking With the King; Life Is a Symphony.

Presentation
There was a c-r-a-s-h of metal against metal with lesser sounds of smashing and banging following. People rushed out to see what had happened. At first all that was apparent was one car with a very badly crumpled front end. But after some searching, the other car was found in a front yard, having smashed through a low wall and some bushes.

Today we're going to talk about wrecks. (Show the car or picture.) Having a car wreck can be very heartbreaking, especially when people are hurt or killed and property is damaged. Cars aren't the only things that can be wrecked, however. To wreck means to ruin or destroy generally, physically, or morally; to pull to pieces. Many things are wrecked on purpose or by carelessness. The type of wrecks we will talk about today cause more heartaches and unhappiness, and have more far-reaching consequences than any other wrecks. We are going to talk about wrecked marriages. Wrecked marriages are tearing down our country. Look ahead, as we talk, and resolve that with God's help, you will build a solid marriage when you take that step in your life.

1. One reason for a car wreck may be a poor instructor or guide. A competent instructor will be well trained and have the welfare of the one he is teaching at heart. He will not give wrong orders and can always be trusted. Although a poor instructor or guide may not account for many wrecks on our highways, a poor instructor is responsible for many wrecked marriages. There is only one Instructor, who has all wisdom, mercy, and power. To have Him at the head of a home is to have real help. Not only does He have wisdom but also love (I John 4:8) and power (Ps. 62:11). What a combination that is!

One great difficulty, though, is that many couples wait until after they're married to ask instruction of God. The time to ask for God's guidance is before marriage. With His approval and help you won't enter an unwise marriage. The Bible says, "Seek ye first the kingdom of God, and his righteousness; and all these things shall be added unto you" (Matt. 6:33).

Another cause for wrecks—both in cars and marriages—is one we don't have to worry about if Christ is our guide. That wrecker is strong drink and drugs.

Another cause for accidents is carelessness and inattention. The driver goes merrily down the road, his mind a thousand miles away. WHAM-OO! He didn't mean to get into that accident. He was just thoughtless. Marriages, too, would be much happier if both parties would remember to be thoughtful of each other. He should remember her birthday, their anniversary, Valentine's day, and give little thoughtful gifts other times, too. He'd appreciate it if she remembered how he liked his egg cooked, when he needs a clean shirt or a button sewed on, and what time he wants dinner. Such thoughtfulness shows love.

Some driving goes beyond carelessness and would have to be written off as reckless driving. Perhaps the driver is speeding or showing off and because of this he loses control of his car. Some of our most serious wrecks come from reckless driving. The reckless driver is more than thoughtless; he is selfish. Selfishness causes wrecks not only on the highways but also in homes. Selfishness means a lack of real love for each other, for love considers others before self. The Bible speaks very plainly about this. In Colossians 3:18, 19 (Living Bible) we read, "You wives, submit yourselves to your husbands, for that is what the Lord has planned for you. And you husbands must be loving and kind to your wives and not bitter against them, nor harsh." The Bible also says, "You husbands must be careful of your wives, being thoughtful of their needs and honoring them as the weaker sex. Remember that you and your wife are partners in receiving God's blessings, and if you don't treat her as you should, your prayers will not get ready answers. You should be like one big happy family, full of sympathy toward each other, loving one another with tender hearts and humble minds" (I Peter 3:7, 8, Living Bible).

There are other times when there is a wreck because of mechanical failure: the brakes don't hold, the tires are worn, or the head light may have burned out. In other words, the car should never have been taken out of the garage. In marriage, I think I'd call that immaturity. Before you take this great step in your life, ask yourself, and ask the Lord, if you are really ready for the responsibilities of building a happy marriage. When the honeymoon is over, will you be able to blend your personality with your mate's in the day-by-day give and take? Will you be able to stand the pressures of earning a living and paying the bills? Are you ready to make the decisions that your parents have been making for you?

Sometimes a car is smashed because of bad road conditions. Many cars have landed upside down in a ditch because of a patch of ice or a combination of rain and oil on the highway. Sometimes these things cannot be avoided, but if the driver is prepared, the results of a skid will be less disastrous. Conditions can sometimes become disastrous in the home, too, without anyone's fault. Someone becomes seriously ill and the bills pile up. The wage earner is laid off the job. If the husband and wife have a firm trust in God, they'll weather the "road conditions" and come out right side up, although they may do some skidding. They will have God's wisdom to draw from. You may also draw from God's mercy and power. He says so in many places. In Deuteronomy 4:31: "(for the Lord thy God is a merciful God;) he will not forsake thee." In Joshua 1:5: "... as I was with Moses, so I will be with thee: I will not fail thee, nor forsake thee." And in I Samuel 12:22: "For the Lord will not forsake his people for his great name's sake." So if trouble comes, hang on and let God's love and your love for each other and for God bring you through and draw you closer together.

In this age of free love and divorces you can be sure God has a better plan, one of happy companionship in marriage. But we must draw from God's wisdom in every situation. God's Word says, "But the wisdom that comes from heaven is first of all pure and full of quiet gentleness. Then it is peace-loving and courteous. It allows discussion and is willing to yield to others; it is full of mercy and good deeds. It is wholehearted and straightforward and sincere" (James 3:17, Living Bible).

14

Phony or Genuine

Objects
A wig, artificial fruit, play money, artificial flowers, and/or other artificial things.

Purpose
To show how we can tell if a religion is false, therefore a cult, and what our stand should be in regard to these cults.

Suggested Songs
Every Promise in the Book Is Mine; I Shall Not Be Moved; I Want God's Way to Be My Way.

Preparation
The following presentation is meant to be primarily a discussion. Be prepared to guide this discussion. You will find the basic answer and the verifying Scripture verse following each discussion question.

Presentation
Have you ever been fooled by something artificial? Today artists are making fakes look so real that one has a difficult time separating the fake from the genuine. (Show the objects you've brought.) Some artificial flowers look so real that we find ourselves smelling them. And people have commented, "Oh, Alice, you cut your hair," only to find that Alice is wearing a wig. Counterfeit money can fool everyone except the experts.

There are also artificial religions which are called cults. As the coming of Jesus draws nearer, more and more of these cults are springing up. These have a certain amount of truth mixed in with their false ideas and this is what makes them so dangerous. People believe the little bit of truth and then fall into the trap of believing the lies woven into the truth. Some of these cults, though, are so close to the truth that it takes someone knowledgeable in God's Word to recognize their false ideas.

(Let the discussion begin here.) How can one tell if a religion is false? (Every part of a doctrine must be backed by the *whole* Bible, rather than only a verse, which could be taken out of context.)

Let us examine a few of these cults in the light of God's Word. Tell me what, according to God's Word, is wrong with the following statements.

(You may or may not want to mention from which cults these statements came. Let the young people decide what the Bible says about the statement. Give them the Bible references to check.)

(Christian Science)

1. Jesus is the human man, and Christ is the divine idea; hence the duality of Jesus the Christ. (*Science and Health,* Mary Baker Eddy, p. 473:15.)

(He is the Son of God: Rom. 1:3, 4.)

2. Man is incapable of sin. (Ibid, p. 475:27)

(All have sinned: Rom. 3:23.)

3. The material blood of Jesus was no more efficacious to cleanse from sin when it was shed upon "the accursed tree," than when it was flowing in his veins. (Ibid, p. 25:6.)

(The blood of Jesus cleanses us from sin: I John 1:7, Matt. 26:28.)

(Jehovah's Witnesses)

1. Jesus Christ was creature inferior to Jehovah, and He did not become a full partaker of the divine nature until after His baptism and death. (Vol. I, *Divine Plan of the Ages,* p. 179)

(He was divine, the Son of God, and with God from the very beginning, and was equal with God: Isa. 9:6; John 1:1-3; Phil. 2:6)

2. The body of Jesus was not resurrected; it was either dissolved in gases, or preserved some place. (Vol. II, *Divine Plan of the Ages,* p. 129.)

(He was seen by numerous people after His resurrection: Luke 24:36-43; I Cor. 15:4-7.)

(Spiritualism)

1. Jesus was not born of a virgin. He was just a medium of high order. *(Isms,* W. T. McLean)

(The Bible says he was born of a virgin: Isa. 7:14; Matt. 1:18. He is the Son of God: Rom. 1:4.)

2. Man becomes his own savior. *(Declaration of Principles.)*

(We are saved through Jesus Christ, not by anything that we do: John 1:12; Eph. 2:8-9.)

3. Hell does not exist and never will. There is no resurrection and no judgment. *(The New Revelation,* p. 68, A. Conan Doyle)

(The Bible says there is a hell: II Peter 2:4; Matt. 25:41. There will be a resurrection and judgment according to the Bible: Dan. 12:2; Heb. 9:27; Rev. 20:12.)

(Unity, School of Christianity)

1. God is not loving. God does not love anybody or anything. God is the love in everybody and everything. *(Jesus Christ Heals,* p. 13, Charles Fillmore.)

(The Bible says that God loves us and the whole world: I John 4:19; John 3:16.)

(Mormons)

1. We believe the Bible to be the Word of God as far as it is translated correctly; we also believe the Book of Mormon to be the Word of God. *(Articles of Faith for the Saints,* No. 8.)

(The Bible is for all men to understand, not just for selected few individuals to interpret, II Peter 1:20. God's Word is simple enough for even children to understand: Isa. 35:8; Luke 10:21; Matt. 11:25. Read the last verse in the Living Bible.)

(God has given direct orders that we are not to add or subtract from God's Word: Deut. 4:2; Rev. 22:18-19.)

Question: Why is it so important to be involved with a religion that follows God's Word *completely*?

(If you cannot believe all of the Bible, you cannot believe *any* of it. How are you to know which part is right and which is wrong? Also, even if you are a strong enough Christian to follow Christ by believing only the correct part of the doctrine of a cult, others who do not know the Bible as well as you do, might be led by you into that church and so be hindered from learning the whole truth about Christ and His kingdom. Furthermore, God's Word says to avoid cults: Rom. 16:17-18.)

Question: How can we know which religion and denomination is right and blessed by God?

(By praying for God's guidance, by studying the Bible to see if that denomination believes the whole Word of God, and by asking counsel of a man you know to be godly. It is dangerous for a person who is not familiar with the Bible to study false religions. Satan's counterfeits are well camouflaged. By taking a verse out of its setting or putting a private interpretation to a text, phony statements can be made to appear like the genuine truth.)

15

Danger, Keep Out!

Objects

Signs reading: Danger—thin ice; Danger—high voltage; Danger—explosives; Danger—Satan's Territory.

Purpose

To acquaint young people with a few of the doors that lead to Satan's territory.

Suggested Songs

Christ for Me; Christ Is the Answer; Follow, I Will Follow Thee; He Set Me Free; Jesus Sets Me Absolutely Free; I'm So Glad Jesus Lifted Me.

Presentation

The sign read: "DANGER—Keep Out!" Bob read it out loud as he and his friend, Skip, paused outside the barricade.

"So what!" was Skip's comment. "That old place has been there for years. It certainly won't topple over now."

True, it didn't fall over, but Bob had to be carried out of the basement on a stretcher after going through the rotten floor. It had been fun ignoring the sign, going over the barricade, and prying some boards off a window. The consequence wasn't fun, however.

DANGER signs are quite common. You'll read: (Hold up the signs and read them.) Why bother with warning signs? To tell people that it is risky to go near that place. Quite often the signs are combined with a STAY OUT sign, too. To disobey those signs is to be foolhardy.

Let's add one more sign now: DANGER—Satan's Territory.

Ever since Satan was asked to leave heaven, he has been setting his traps to lure God's children into his territory and to bind his own more securely, such traps as: fear, discouragement, procrastination, or putting things off. It seems that Satan is becoming more bold today, perhaps because he realizes that his time is short. And as people become disgusted with world political and economic affairs, more and more of them are joining wholeheartedly with Satan. Satan is making his cause seem so desirable, but once a person is trapped, Satan's chains are almost unbreakable, except by the power of God. Let's look into some of the territories of Satan. Most of Satan's paths are well camouflaged.

1. Astrology and horoscopes are two paths into Satan's territory. There is some truth in astrology—and that is what makes it so dangerous. The little bit of truth hooks people and they fail to see the tons of lies that are connected to the thin thread of truth.

What is astrology? Webster says it is the pseudo-science of prediction by means of the stars and other heavenly bodies. Astrologers claim that they can predict events on earth by the position of the moon, sun, fixed stars, and planets. But notice, astrology isn't called science but *pseudo*-science which means false or counterfeit. Don't confuse astrology with astronomy, a real science which studies the heavenly bodies.

Some Christians believe God is the power behind the predictions of astrology. But remember, when God predicts something, He will be 100 percent right. Though you don't often hear about it, all astrologers miss in their predictions a great many times. For example, astrologers warned that in April, 1969, California would have a terrible earthquake and either a large part or the whole state would land in the Pacific Ocean. Several Aprils have since passed but California is still there. On October 20, 1968, Jeanne Dixon's syndicated column had to be hurriedly withdrawn from newspapers. She had said that she did not see any marriage for Jackie Kennedy in the near future. That column would have appeared in the same issue of the paper that announced the wedding of Jacqueline Kennedy and Aristotle Onassis.

Why is astrology evil? First, because God said so. In the Old Testament God ordered those who worshiped the stars to be stoned (Deut. 17:2-5). Isaiah classed astrology along with other false religions (Isa. 47:12, 13). Secondly, astrology looks to man and the stars, rather than to God, to find direction for life and the steps of the day. That is making a god of the stars and God has commanded: "Thou shalt have no other gods before me" (Exod. 20:3).

Many people go to the daily horoscope before they make any decisions. But take an objective look at daily horoscopes and you'll see that they are written in such a vague way that they could mean almost anything.

So, stay away from astrology. Satan is the force behind it and any steps into his territory result in weaving Satan's cord more tightly about us.

2. Another atractive lure that Satan has for getting us into his territory is the Ouija (or yes-yes) board. It is supposed to be just a game, but when you are playing it, you're actually playing a game with Satan and his evil spirits.

This board has the alphabet, the numerals from zero to nine, yes, no, and goodbye on it. The players lightly put their fingers on the plastic disk. Then as a question is asked the board points to letters or numbers and spells out the answer. Nicky Cruz in his book, *Satan on the Loose,* tells how a group of young people asked the board to name the spirit working it. The plants in the room began to sway and the piano began to tinkle. When a young lady realized that she wasn't just playing a game, she dropped to her knees in prayer and the Ouija board disk quickly spun to goodbye and bounced off the table onto the floor.

Stay away from this innocent appearing game—it's Satan's property.

3. Another trap of Satan is the cult, spiritualism. Spiritualists believe that there can be communication between the dead and the living through a medium. Thousands are joining this cult because it looks so interesting. But the magic is just the power of Satan. Some members of this cult will say that they are drawn closer to God by speaking with the dead. That is impossible, for one can be drawn to God only through Jesus

Christ (John 14:6). Spiritualists deny that Jesus was anything more than a medium of high order. They also say that Jesus was not divine. God warned against this cult in Deuteronomy 18:9-11.

Once a son who was a medium, begged his mother to come to a seance, as the spiritualist meetings are called. She finally agreed. But before she went, she spent much time in prayer and continued praying even during the seance. The son finally had to call the meeting to a halt and told everyone to go home for, as he said, "Someone here is working against us." God, the stronger Spirit, had taken control.

4. Another way to go into Satan's territory is through transcendental meditation. Members of this cult practice clearing their minds of all thoughts and, supposedly, wait for God to fill their minds with thoughts from Him. Some say that this is their way to God. What is wrong with that? Jesus said, "I am the door" (John 10:9). Also, "I am the way—no man cometh unto the Father, but by me" (John 14:6). Secondly, it won't be God's Spirit that will take possession of an empty mind. He comes in only by invitation; He is a gentleman. Satan is no gentleman: he pushes his way in through any crack he can find.

Satan is holding up many other cults, hoping to attract you by their flashy but deadly lure. There is the crystal ball, ESP, hynosis, modern theology, Hare Krishna, magic, reincarnation.

Many people are *not* going into Satan's territory through what we might call the back door. They are marching in directly through Satan worship and witchcraft. How terrible. They are inviting Satan to bind them and he never binds with love but with fear, hatred, and oppression. He has nothing to offer but a broken mind, broken body, and eternal life spent with him in hell.

Stay away from Satan's territory! Don't enter in through either the back or front door. Both doors offer D-A-N-G-E-R. Someday Satan and his followers will fight God and the saints. If you're on Satan's side, you're on the losing side. Join the winners.

16

Are You Running on Empty?

Objects
A picture of a car's gas gauge with the needle pointing to EMPTY, other things which are either completely empty or nearly so, such as a pen, shampoo bottle, a tube of toothpaste, etc.

Purpose
To show the need of being filled and staying filled with the Spirit.

Suggested Songs
Filled with God; Be Filled with the Spirit; Give Me Oil in My Lamp; He Will Fill Your Heart Today; If Any Man Thirst.

Presentation
During the time of shortages, frustrations build. It's frustrating to get your head wet and then find that you're out of shampoo. It's frustrating to be in the middle of a test and then have your pen run dry. (Show the empty containers as you talk.)

It's worse to be on the highway fifty miles from nowhere, and discover that your gas gauge registers EMPTY.

Is there any other warning that we're going to be left sitting beside the highway other than the gas gauge needle pointing to EMPTY? Quite often there is. There is some sputtering and missing, especially as the car goes up a hill.

Worse than an empty gas tank on a car is the Christian whose spiritual gas tank is almost empty. Let me quickly say, however, that his spiritual emptiness isn't because of a shortage of supply; rather that Christian hasn't gone to the *source* of supply.

How can one read his spiritual gas gauge? If you have a

godly love for everyone, even the ungodly, if you have a desire to see others won for Christ, if you have a desire to pray and read God's Word, your "gas tank" probably has a good amount of "gas."

There are other signs. If you can live the Christian life only when everything is favorable, if you spit and sputter when you can't have your own way or someone doesn't think you are the "most," if you don't have power to live like Jesus when you're among the unsaved, beware! These are all signs of a nearly empty spiritual gas tank.

Of course, the big danger of running on a nearly empty gas tank is that you won't get to the place you wish to go. And for the Christian, the spiritual application is rather shattering, for who wants to even consider not making it to heaven.

The Bible tells about ten virgins (Matt. 25:1-13) who were waiting to escort the bridegroom to the home of the bride. Each virgin had her lamp burning. The bridegroom, however, didn't come when the ladies expected him, so five virgins ran out of oil.

The followers of Christ are like these virgins. We've lighted our spiritual lamps and are shining for Jesus. But though we know Jesus is coming to earth to take us back with Him, He isn't coming as soon as we thought He would. So we go ahead with this business of living.

There is nothing wrong about doing the things that are needful while we're waiting for Christ to come *if* we make sure our hearts are ready at all times for His coming. The Bible says that five of the virgins were wise, they were ready for their bridegroom. Five foolishly figured the oil they had put in their lamps was sufficient; they didn't need to look ahead. That was their big mistake. It would be the same as if we decided it was enough just to have prayed six months ago. To have asked Christ a year ago to give us a clean heart and put His Spirit in us is not enough to keep us in readiness for that great marriage supper of the Lamb that the Bible speaks about in Revelation 19:7-9. Keeping filled with the Spirit is a day-by-day task. To neglect to pray or to read your Bible for even a few days will soon result in your running nearly empty, spiritually speaking.

The five foolish virgins realized their mistake of not being prepared as they waited. They tried to get some extra oil from the wise virgins but the wise virgins couldn't give them any oil. The foolish virgins had to go to the source themselves, and they waited too long to do that, for by the time they had oil, the door to the great celebration was closed and they were left outside.

We, too, cannot depend on others to get us to heaven; we must do our own praying, our own receiving from Christ. Just because you belong to *(name of your church)*, and have a wonderful pastor by the name of *(name of pastor)*, doesn't mean that he's going to be able to take you all to heaven as a group. Being ready is an individual task.

If you feel that your gauge is reading empty, what should you do? Perhaps we can learn from this story. A little boy had just come from Sunday school and was headed for home on an open street car. In his hand he held a card he had received. It was a very precious possession to him and he had very proudly learned the Bible portion on the bottom: "Have faith in God." As he was looking at it this way and that, the card somehow slipped from his hands and the breeze whirled it into the street. The cry that followed could be heard all over the street car: "Oh, I've lost my 'faith in God'! Stop the car! Stop the car, please!" The good-natured conductor pulled over and let the little boy pick up his "faith in God" while adults smiled.

Smile if you like, but that little boy had the right idea. Anyone who has lost something as precious as his faith in God should stop, go back, and pick it up. Not necessarily at the same spot but through communication with God, ask Him to give once again the belief he once had in Him, and fill him with His Spirit.

So, if you're running on empty, go to the source of spiritual help and ask to be filled with God's Spirit once again.

17

Three Cheers

Objects

Three megaphones. (see preparation section)

Purpose

To remind the young people of how great it is to be a Christian.

Suggested Songs

I'm Glad I'm a Christian; I Will Sing of the Mercies; I'm So Glad I Belong to Jesus; Oh, Say but I'm Glad; I've Got Something.

Preparation

Make three megaphones from heavy paper. Write one of the following on each: forgiveness, companionship and help, and victory.

Presentation

Today I have three megaphones for three cheers. By the time I'm through, I'm hoping that each of you will be ready to give three cheers.

If you have the old school spirit, it's not hard to cheer the home team. Even if the team should lose, school loyalty keeps spirits up while you say, "OK, so they *did* lose this game; we still have the best team, and they'll win next time."

Sometimes it is rather hard to cheer, especially if you're not sure there is anything to cheer for. That is the way it is with the Christian life. Some people think it is a gloomy, down-in-the-mouth type of life. But I want to show you three cheers of the Bible and I hope each of you will be ready to give three cheers for belonging to Jesus before you go home.

The first cheer is for forgiveness. (Show each megaphone as you talk about it.) Some men brought to Jesus a man who had palsy. Jesus saw their faith and, putting the most important thing first, He said, "Son, be of good cheer; thy sins be forgiven thee."

No one likes to have a guilty conscience, and if he knows that punishment is certain, he feels worse. Anyone who has sin in his life is sure to have a guilty conscience. Oh, he might try to talk himself out of it, but the Bible says, "All have sinned and come short of the glory of God" (Rom. 3:23). Not only do we have that terrible feeling of sin, but we also know that sin has to be punished. This feeling of doom can certainly make us feel unhappy, for the Bible says, "The wages of sin is death" (Rom. 6:23a).

A young man had lived a terrible life. Finally he left home and broke off all ties with his family. One day he heard that his father had passed away. This influenced him to return home. When he arrived, his mother greeted him lovingly. The day came for the reading of the will. Everyone in the family was present while a lawyer read the document. To the surprise of everyone, the first part of the will was a detailed account of the wayward acts of this particular son. Finally, in anger, the son got up, stamped out of the room, and left home again. After three years, he learned that he had been left $15,000. He had heard only the first part of the will; he hadn't waited to hear the last. Yes, the Bible does say, "The wages of sin is death," but then it goes on to say, "but the gift of God is eternal life through Jesus Christ our Lord" (Rom. 6:23). And that is enough to make us cheer.

A minister was becoming annoyed with one of his members who was constantly going about saying, "Glory!" "Hallelujah!" and "Praise the Lord!" One day the minister invited the man for lunch and, to keep him from praising the Lord all the time, gave him a science book to read. The minister was sure that would be so dull that the man would not find anything in there for which to praise the Lord. In a few minutes the minister heard him shouting, "Glory!" "Hallelujah!" "Praise the Lord!" "What's that all about?" the minister asked. "Why, this book says the sea is five miles deep. And the Bible says my sins have been cast into the depths of the sea. If the sea is that deep, I need not be afraid of my sins ever coming up again. Glory!"

If you have asked Jesus to forgive you your sins, be happy. He's done it! You will never have to worry about them again. The Bible says, "Blessed, and to be envied—are those whose sins are forgiven and put out of sight. Yes, what joy there is for anyone whose sins are no longer counted against him" (Rom. 6:7, 8, Living Bible). So—ONE CHEER!

The second cheer is for companionship and help.

The disciples were in a ship at night and the wind came up, tossing the waves high. Jesus came to them, walking on the waves. What a frightening situation to be in! First a terrible storm, and then a spirit (or so they thought) walking on the water. But Jesus said, "Be of good cheer; it is I; be not afaraid" (Matt. 14:27).

Now isn't *that* something to be happy about? Two things in one verse. First, we have companionship, a real friend who loves us, one who is with us all the time, even in impossible situations and impossible places. Some of the last words Jesus said on earth were: "And, lo, I am with you alway, even unto the end of the world" (Matt. 28:20). Now wasn't that an odd time to say that He was always going to be with the disciples? He said those words just before He went to heaven. He knew that His Spirit would always be with them even after He did go to His Father in heaven. And the message is the same for His twentieth-century disciples. We never need to be alone or lonely. Now that is something to cheer about!

That verse in Matthew 14:27 has something else to cheer about, too. It says, "Be of good cheer; it is I; *be not afraid.*" As long as we have Christ with us, we have no need to be afraid, even of things which look frightening. For example, that first day at a new school among strangers, or the speech you have to make, or the solo you must sing, or the first day on that new job, or—you add the rest of the *ors* to fit your own fears. His promises are so many and include the supplying of our physical, spiritual, and material needs.

It is usually the unknown that makes us afraid. There was once an Englishman who was employed in forestry in India. He woke up suddenly from an afternoon nap under the trees to see his pet fox terrier, Ruffie, barking away at a large bull elephant who had wandered that way. The elephant stood there for a few moments, then turned tail, and ran for all it was worth. It had been frightened by the tiny fox terrier. The unknown usually is nothing to be afraid of, and with Christ we can always "Be not afraid." Another CHEER!

The third cheer is based on John 16:33 (read). I'd call this the victory cheer. Too many times people have said, "I'd be a Christian if I were sure I'd be able to stick it out." If you've said that, you're very wrong. Paul has said—and we can say too—"I can do all things through Christ which strengtheneth me" (Phil. 4:13). Paul also said, "And I am sure that God who began the good work within you will keep right on helping you grow in His grace until His task within you is finally finished on that day when Jesus Christ returns" (Phil. 1:6, Living Bible). We were saved through Christ Jesus. He started it. And we will be kept by Christ Jesus. He will finish it. We are on the winning side. True, Satan does try to make us stumble and desert the winning side but, "Greater is he that is in you, than he that is in the world" (I John 4:4b). Satan will try to get us on his side, and by ourselves we would get knocked about but with Christ on our side we will win.

A story is told of an ugly old tug nicknamed *Bust-Me-Up* which ran between London and Portsmouth. It seemed that everytime she came into port, she collided with a boat and did some damage. That's how she got the name *Bust-Me-Up*. One day she surprised everyone and came in straight and true, gliding gracefully into her berth. A sailor standing on the dock couldn't believe his eyes and shouted, "Whatever's come over you, old *Bust-Me-Up?*" The answer came back from a deck hand, "A new skipper on board."

If we try to go through life without the one and only winning Skipper, we're going to feel and, perhaps look, like old *Bust-Me-Up*. When Christ Jesus pilots our life, He gives us the strength and ability to get the best from life and to enter heaven with a shout.

Are you ready to give three cheers? Then let's give them—for forgiveness, companionship, and victory—all through Christ Jesus our Lord. Aren't you glad that you're a Christian?

(End by singing, Isn't It Grand to Be a Christian.)

18

Don't Be an Octopus

Objects
As many pictures as you can get of octopus, squid, and cuttlefish.

Purpose
To encourage all who have difficulty being loyal to Jesus to pray and to let their Christian colors shine.

Suggested Songs
I Am Determined; To Be Like Jesus; Stand Fast Therefore in the Liberty; Keep Me True, Lord Jesus.

Presentation
We're going to talk about an interesting creature of God's creation pictured here. Naturally, in this short time we can't learn all there is to know about the octopus because thousands of pages have been written about him. Because we want to use this eight-armed oddity to bring out some spiritual comparisons, we'll zero in on his personality—if an octopus has a personality—and the techniques he uses to keep from getting caught.

Before going into any octopus stories, I want to make a rather startling statement: every Christian at one time or another has behaved somewhat like an octopus. For an octopus to act like an octopus is fine, but for a person to act like an octopus, *that* is *not* fine. Some Christians put on this octopus act when they don't want others to know or recognize them as Christians. Let's go back to the octopus and I'm sure you'll see what I mean.

The octopus doesn't seem to be too sociable. He loves to hide. Nothing too unusual there except that they hide or live in odd places. Frank Lane in his book, *Kingdom of the Octo-*

pus,[1] tells about a Royal Navy diver named Henry Bruce who went searching for a torpedo in the waters off Gibraltar. He didn't find the torpedo but he did find a suit of overalls. Without too much thought, he grabbed one of the arms and then was horrified as the overalls seemed to come to life. They raised up and swayed like some ballet dancer. He was petrified with fright until an arm reached out and wrapped itself around his ankle. This quickly put some life back into Bruce for he knew what was "wearing" those overalls. There was quite a fight between Bruce and an octopus. Happily, Bruce, with the aid of a knife, won.

His habit of hiding in things very often gets the octopus into trouble and captured. Men who want to catch the octopus sink jars and pots into the water, knowing that in all probability the octopus will go inside to hide. Then they pull up the pot and they've got one unhappy octopus.

Sometimes Christians are so afraid of being different or being made fun of that they stay off to themselves. That way there will be no danger of having to say "No" to some temptation or to stand out in the crowd as being different. To shy away from others because we don't want others to know which side we're on will soon bring us trouble, however. Satan can use this fear to bring discouragement and condemnation. Not only will this make us miserable, but it may also be the wedge Satan uses to get us back on his side.

Another reason why many Christians stay off by themselves is that they consider themselves too good to associate with sinners. This is not right, either. The word *Christian* means to be Christ-like, so let's use Christ as our example. What did He do while He was here on earth? He had every right to consider Himself as being too righteous to mingle with sinners. We see Him associating with all types of people. If He had stayed only with the Christians, He would not have had many followers. It was by associating with people that they felt His love, compassion, and righteousness.

---

1. Frank W. Lane, *Kingdom of the Octopus,* New York: Sheridan House, 1960

Christ's closest friends, of course, were His disciples (and I don't mean just the twelve). Like Christ, we too should mingle with the unsaved but our closest friends should be fellow Christians. Jesus said, "And ye shall be witnesses unto me" (Acts 1:8). To be a witness, we must go among the people.

Another habit the octopus has is not being where you expect to find him, or being where you *don't* expect to find him. He's quite an escape artist. He seems to almost melt through little spaces several times smaller in diameter than he is. This can be very disturbing to many people. Another amusing story comes from Frank Lane's *Kingdom of the Octopus*. He relates the incident of an octopus, about a foot long, which had been captured and was being carried home on a bus in a wicker basket. In about ten minutes there was a hysterical scream. The man quickly went to the rescue of both the passenger and the octopus who was draped over the passenger's lap. The octopus had squeezed through a half-inch crack to make his escape.

Sometimes followers of Christ are found in places you would hardly expect them to be found or they are absent from places where you would expect to find them. Suppose you're with a group of kids and they say, "Hey, let's go and see a movie." You know it is not a good movie but because you don't want them to think you're a square, you go along, even though you know you're not pleasing your Savior. Or suppose you're spending the weekend away from home. Rather than go to church by yourself and be labeled as being different, you stay home with the rest. Such actions are in obedience to an alien master. We're putting ourselves in danger—spiritual danger.

One of the best techniques the octopus has for protection is his ability to change color in a fraction of a second. He and his two first cousins, the squid and cuttlefish, do this by means of tiny pigment or color cells. These cells expand and contract to regulate the color of the octopus. For example, if he wishes to be brown, the brown pigment cells expand. Although the cells are very tiny, they can be expanded up to sixty times. This would be the same as if a two-inch high rat in a flash became as large as a ten-foot elephant. The quick color change is controlled by muscles. Octopuses tend to change the color to blend in with their background situation.

To further confuse their enemies, octopuses give off an inky substance which provides a dark screen. *Kingdom of the Octopus* tells of a zoologist named Hall who tried to catch a three-inch squid in a tub. When his hand got about nine inches from the squid, the squid changed to a dark color and seemed to stand still. When Mr. Hall tried to grab it, his hand went through just a blob of ink. He discovered the squid on the other side of the tub. Mr. Hall tried again and watched what happened. He discovered that the squid, all in a second, ejected some dark ink about his size, turned pale, and darted away.

The prize for the ability to match their background colorwise would seem to go to the cuttlefish. One was put in a black tub, and it turned black. Then it was put in a white tub and it turned as pale as a cuttlefish can. Then it was put in a black tub that had a white square on the bottom. The color change wasn't perfect but the cuttlefish certainly tried. It became all black except for a white dot at the rear, a white band across its head, and—a white square in the middle.

The octopus not only changes his color to match his home but also at times changes the texture of his skin. An octopus can look as if he has seaweed attached to his back.

Yes, the octopus and his family, the cephalopods, are very interesting to study. An octopus has every right to act like an octopus. But Christians have no right to act like an octopus. When some Christians are around other Christians in church or at home, they take on the mannerisms of a Christian, but when they get around the unsaved crowd at school or elsewhere, they seem to "change color." They don't seem to have the backbone to be different from the world. Now I'm quite sure it makes the octopus feel better—more safe and secure—after he's changed color. But you'll have to admit, if you've ever "changed color," that you felt guilty, you know you're turning your back on your best Friend by being ashamed to acknowledge that you belong to Him. (Read Mark 8:38.) Jesus knew you'd have trouble. While He was here on earth,

He lovingly prayed to His Heavenly Father for you. (Read John 17:15-20, Living Bible.) So, if you're having "octopus trouble," *you* pray to your Heavenly Father too. He'll help you have the backbone, which an octopus doesn't have, to stand up for Jesus and proudly say, "I belong to the family of God."

19

A Good Old Soul or a Miserable Heel

Object
A shoe with a fairly good sole, but having a run-down heel with nails showing below the rubber and above in the shoe lining.

Purpose
From the Proverbs of Solomon we can be assured that the rewards of the righteous far outweigh any brief pleasures of the wicked.

Suggested Songs
Something Happened When He Saved Me; Make Me a Blessing; I've Got Peace Like a River; I'm So Glad I Belong to Jesus.

Presentation
Today I brought a shoe. As you take a good look at each end of it, I want to ask you a question. "Are you a good old soul or a miserable heel?" If you are like one end of the shoe, you will be a blessing and people will love to be around you. But if you're like the other end of the shoe, you spell T-R-O-U-B-L-E.

Let's look first at the heel, and compare it to those who do not follow Christ. Those following Satan will be either miserable themselves or make everyone else miserable.

First, I want you to notice that the heel certainly isn't very nice to look at; it is run-down, uneven, dirty, and scuffed. A person following Satan isn't too nice to look at either. Oh, I'll grant you, he may be beautiful, or handsome, in physical features, but he will be lacking in inner beauty. Inner beauty comes only with a loving personality. Some unsaved people can have a wonderful personality and be liked and respected. But in God's sight their beauty is marred by the stains of sin. And the greatest sin of all is rejecting God's Son.

This heel certainly doesn't make the wearer very comfortable, in fact, quite the opposite. For one thing, he can't walk straight. There are nails to prick and puncture his feet. Those following Satan don't walk very straight either. A wicked person is certainly hard on those around him. He's hard to get along with. Many times his ways, attitudes, and words make him disgusting to be around. Solomon has much to say about the "miserable heel" and the "good-old-soul." One proverb which fits in so well here is: "A rebellious son is a grief to his father and a bitter blow to his mother" (Prov. 17:25, Living Bible).

Anyone wearing this kind of a shoe is sure to be slowed down in his walking. If he's with a group, he will slow them down too. A wicked person often is a hindrance to those about him. Perhaps you've been in a class when the teacher said, "As soon as everyone is quiet, we'll be dismissed." And though there is 99 percent quietness, there is always that one who wants to show off. Because of him or her the whole class has to stay longer.

This miserable heel is hard to have around any place. As an employee, he's a deadweight. Solomon said, "A lazy fellow is a pain to his employers." As a marriage partner, he or she makes life hectic, too. Solomon says, "A worthy wife is her husband's joy and crown, the other kind corrodes his strength and tears down everything he does" (Prov. 12:4, Living Bible). Yes, Solomon was really with it when he said, "A man with a warped mind is despised" (Prov. 12:8b, Living Bible).

This kind of a heel can not only be a pain in the foot but a "pain in the neck" as well. He spells disaster in too many places. The protruding nails in the heel catch on the loops in the shag rug and scratch deep marks on hard surface floors. In the same way, wickedness leaves behind it sadness and destruction. The only person that really likes to be around such a heel is someone just like him. Again, back to Solomon and see what he has to say. (Have read, preferably in Living Bible, the following verses: Prov. 13:20; 14:29; 15:1; 16:28, 29; 17:12.)

Now let's go to the other end of the shoe, and see the "good old soul" (sole). It is just the opposite from the miserable heel. It is smooth, wearable, not too bad to look at. It bends when it needs to, has plenty of wear left, and gets the wearer around. So it is with the "good old souls." They go about doing their work and many times the work of others. They're not causing a lot of friction and hard feelings while they do it. They're a joy to be with and work with. Back to Solomon to see what he has to say about the "good old souls." (Read, preferably from Living Bible: Prov. 11:11; 12:4a; 12:8a; 13:20a; 16:7; 17:22a.)

Maybe you think the life of the "good old souls" is very uninteresting, but you are wrong. They're on their way to a happy, full life here on earth, and then heaven to come. They're not being held back by bad habits and Christ helps them with the irritable things that makes them disgusted with others. Then they have the satisfaction of knowing they are helping others.

A young lady came to church saying that she wanted to join. As the trustees talked to her, they became convinced that she was a truly sincere Christian. They asked her who it was who had led her to Christ. She told them, "Dr. S." They said, "Oh, you are a friend of his?"

"No," she replied, "I have never met him or even seen him."

The puzzled minister asked how she was led to Christ by the Christian doctor.

She told them that she was a telephone operator and had night duty from nine in the evening until three in the morning. Many times, she said, she had to awaken Dr. S. in the middle of the night. Several times she had rung his number by mistake. "But," she said, "he always answered with courtesy and with a voice that showed no impatience. He was so different from the others that answered. They were angry, discourteous, and peevish—especially if I should wake them by mistake."

So she started asking around to find out what the difference was and discovered that Dr. S. belonged to Christ and lived so close to Him that Christ was reflected in Dr. S.'s relations with everyone. The telephone operator accepted this same Jesus as her Savior.

Come and join the "good old souls." Don't be a miserable heel.

20

This Great Body

Object
The speaker himself is the object.

Purpose
To show that Christ wants all of us to be one body, in love, with Him at the center.

Suggested Songs
We Are One; Let Us Break Bread Together; Just a Closer Walk with Thee; Every Moment of Every Day.

Presentation
Ned looked at his right hand. "Dirty again," he muttered disgustedly. "I'm tired of washing it all the time; I think I'll cut it off and get rid of it."

Of course you know that wouldn't happen. No one would be that foolish.

Jesus said all His followers together make up the body of Christ. Just as your hand is part of your body, so each of you is part of the body of Christ. We read about it in I Corinthians 12:12-21. (Read from Living Bible.)

Let's think about these bodies that God has so wonderfully made and compare them with Christians, or the body of Christ.

First, the parts of a human body are different sizes and look different, one from the other. (Point to the various parts as you talk.) My mouth isn't nearly as big as my arm, neither is my ear shaped like my foot. It is easy to see that in this great family of God, there are people of all sizes, too—big like your parents, smaller like your little brothers and sisters, fat, skinny.

In your body, too, there are parts you can see and parts you can't see. You can't see your lungs, but just try to do without them. Your mouth might say, "Everyone can see me when beautiful music comes out of me. I'm much more important than the lungs." But of course we know that no music at all would come from the mouth unless the lungs were doing their job. In the same way, a Christian may have a work for Jesus where everyone sees him, but many times someone is praying, quietly and unknown, for the one who is performing. That person is so very important to the body of Christ.

What would you think if your ears should say to your eyes, "You're not the same color as I am, so you're not very important." Silly, isn't it? And it is just as silly to say that because a person is from a different race and has a different color, he isn't as important as you are in the family of God.

Now let me ask you a question. What happens when you get in a car and someone slams the door on your finger?

Your whole body sympathizes with that one little finger. Your mouth says, "Ouch!" Tears may come to your eyes. You probably grab your finger with your other hand, and shake it or cradle it while you moan and groan.

That is how it should be in the body of Christ. (Read I Cor. 12:26, Living Bible.) If one member is feeling badly because of something that has happened, others should be a special friend to that one and pray for him.

Now suppose one part of your body is weaker than it should be, for example, your eyes. What do you do then? (Rest them, see an eye doctor, wear glasses.) We give them extra special care.

Sometimes one Christian may seem weaker than the others. Perhaps it is because he hasn't had Christian parents to help him as some others have. (Read I Cor. 12:22, Living Bible.) If you know of a person who has difficulty living as Jesus would have him live, you should rally round and be a special friend to him and pray for him. Just because he's weak doesn't mean that he doesn't have a very important place in the family of God.

Another thing happens to our bodies sometimes. We become careless and really hurt ourselves. For example, Don didn't watch where he was going while he was carrying a glass. He tripped and fell breaking the glass, and, worse yet, severely gashing his arm. The first thing he's going to do is rush to his parents and get their help. They will probably put on a temporary bandage and rush him to the doctor for some stitches. Every part of Don's body feels terrible because Don was careless.

Sad to say, this is also what happens sometimes to the members of God's family. They become careless and don't pray and read their Bible enough so they slip and do something displeasing to God. It is wonderful to know, however, that our loving Heavenly Father forgives when they come to Him.

Several things can happen, besides a person getting hurt. First, when Don came to his mother, what was the first thing she saw? (His cut arm.) She didn't see the arm that wasn't cut. And this is the way it seems to be when someone does something displeasing to the Lord, such as stealing. Those who are not Christians don't see all the other Christians that have never stolen. They see only the one who does. Of course, that isn't the way it should be—but it is. Then just as Don's whole body felt bad when he was cut, so the whole body of Christ suffers, too.

And last, what will probably be left on Don's arm even after it heals? (A scar.) Yes, and that is also what sin leaves many times. Suppose this person who stole something never does it again. Yet others are going to wonder, "Can I trust him?" And those outside the family of God may say, "If that is the way Christians are, I don't want to be one." Scars aren't very nice to have. We should pray for those who have sinned, that God will heal their scars very soon. Let us also remember that God can use those members in His family in spite of the scars. So don't look down on them, just pray for them.

God's Word says: (read I Cor. 12:27, Living Bible). Let us treat this great body of Christ as we would our own body and let us always remember that Christ should always have the most important part as the very center of and guide to our actions.

21

I Have a Bone to Pick with You

Objects
Five bones

Purpose
If their youth group seems dull and dead, to help the young people to take a good look at themselves in the light of God's Word.

Suggested Songs
Jesus, Use Me; He'll Put a Light in Your Eye; Christ Is the Answer; Create in Me a Clean Heart.

Preparation
Attach one of the following name tags to each of the five bones: lazy bone, funny bone, bone of contention, wishbone, and backbone.

Presentation
The Bible tells of the prophet Ezekiel who was given a vision from God (Ezek. 37). It almost seems to be a nightmare. He saw a valley full of dry bones. In his vision God told him, "Go, talk to these dry bones and tell them to hear my words. Tell them I'm going to put life in them once again."

After Ezekiel had given the message to the bones, he heard a rattling sound as the bones began to move. The skulls moved over and attached themselves to the vertebra. The bones of the hands and arms came together and then snapped into the shoulder bone. Oh, what a noise as all the bones came together. Then the rattling stopped and muscles and flesh began to appear on the bones and lastly, skin made the final covering.

There was still something missing, however. The bones were just some dead corpses lying out in the sun. Then God told Ezekiel to call to the four winds to blow upon these bodies and breathe life into them again. As Ezekiel did what he was told, the winds came and soon each body stood to its feet—and, lo! a living army appeared.

God told Ezekiel that these bones represented Israel, exiled with all hope gone. But God promised Israel hope of wonderful things to come. Of course, He wasn't going to force all these things on them; they would still have to accept them and put their trust in Him. But what a wonderful future they had: life, hapipness, and even the hope of the Messiah.

I wonder if sometimes our youth group feels like these dry bones. Perhaps we feel that there is no hope—nothing seems to happen. Could it be that we need to let God do some work on these bones and put in new life?

I've brought some bones with me and named them. Let's see if we have some of them here in person. Hopefully not, but if we do, let us see what God has to say to them.

First, we have this bone, (show each bone as you talk about it) and I've named it the *lazy bone*. Lazy bones in our youth group are sure to make our services and projects dead. If Sam refuses to help decorate for the senior banquet, if Edith can't miss her favorite TV show to visit the rest home, and if Bob sits slouched in his chair with his eyes closed during the song service, everything is sure to be less lively than if they took part. Not only are we minus that one person's cooperation, but he influences the rest of the group. Let's see what the Lord has to say to lazy bones.

The Bible says in Hebrews 6:12, "be not slothful, but followers of them who through faith and patience inherit the promises." God's Word becomes a little plainer yet when it says, "Never be lazy in your work but serve the Lord enthusiastically" (Rom. 12:11, Living Bible). If we follow this verse the Lord promises, "After a while we will reap a harvest of blessing if we don't get discouraged and give up" (Gal. 6:9b, Living Bible). So if there are any lazy bones here, get to rattling and serve the Lord enthusiastically.

Next, I have the *funny bone*. Sometimes they call this the crazy bone. The funny bones might keep things lively during the youth services but certainly in the wrong way. Nothing will be accomplished in the right sense; no young people won for Jesus and made ready for heaven. There is nothing wrong in laughing and having fun, but as Ecclesiastes says, there is a time for everything, even "a time to laugh" (Eccles. 3:4). But worshiping God, and learning things about living the Christian life and getting ready for heaven is no joking matter. True, it is a joyful life and happiness wells up within us as we truly worship the Lord. But the funny or crazy bones aren't showing the joy of Christ but rather the light foolishness that is placed there by Satan who wishes our minds to be kept from thinking about his enemy, the Lord Jesus Christ.

In the Old Testament times, worship was so serious that there was great preparation. One account was given in Exodus 19:10, 11. (Read.) We no longer follow the pattern of Old Testament worship but still we should prepare our hearts and minds to think of Him if we wish Christ's joy and blessings on our life, and a new life of happiness for other young people as they accept Him, too. If there are any funny bones present, let's pray that they, too, will start rattling with new spiritual life.

The next bone I have is the *bone of contention*. The word *contention* means quarrelsomeness. How quarreling can kill the spiritual life and make things look hopeless! Sue says, "Let's sit back here; I just can't *stand* Becky." And John says, "Bill and his bunch always get what they want; we were supposed to go bowling this time.' And so it goes, hard feelings, angry words, grumbling, and the Holy Spirit seems to be tied. What actually is happening, however, is that we are so filled with our attitude of bitterness and anger that Christ cannot speak to us, and our attitude influences others. And as Proverbs 17:14 says, "It is hard to stop a quarrel once it starts, so don't let it begin" (Living Bible). Let's see what else the Word of the Lord has to say to these bones.

The Bible says, "If it be possible, as much as lieth in you, live peaceably with all men" (Rom. 12:18). It also says, "try to live in peace with everyone; work hard at it" (Ps. 34:14b,

Living Bible). God is not the author of confusion and hatefulness, but rather of love. The Bible says, "Beloved, let us love one another" (I John 4:7).

Can I hear the rattling of some more bones, moving closer together?

Here is a bone which I've called the *wishbone*. There is nothing wrong with wishing. The difficulty comes when we stop working and do nothing but wishing. We can wish from now until the Atlantic Ocean dries up for our young people's room to be redecorated, but unless we roll up our sleeves and do something about it, it will stay as dingy as it is. We can wish for more young people to attend our meetings and be won to Christ, but unless we do some praying and then "put feet to our prayers" there probably will be no change.

We can believe that God is going to make our youth group more profitable, but unless we help this to come about, it probably won't. James 2:17 says, "Faith, if it hath not works, is dead, being alone."

Wishbones, follow I Corinthians 15:58. (Read.) Do I hear some more rattling?

Yes, these four bones: the lazy bones, the funny bones, the bones of contention, and the wishbones bring hopelessness and death to our youth activities. Rather than get rid of the bones, let's "hear the word of the Lord" and come to spiritual life. Become a bone which is part of the body of Christ. In other words, how about becoming the backbone of the church? Then you'll be used to bring new life to the group.

22

Be My Valentine

Objects
A Bible covered with paper, a colored heart on both the front and back. Sixteen large valentine hearts with one of the following printed on each: MY LOVE, TRUE LOVE, WOW!, MY BOY and MY GIRL, SAY YES, HAPPY, LOVE KNOT, NO, ASK DAD, ASK ME, KEEP STILL, SURE CAN, TRUE BLUE, BIG DEAL, LET'S FLY, WILL YOU?

Purpose
To foster a greater love for God and His Son as we think of their great love for us.

Suggested Songs
Can You Wonder; His Love Hath No Limit; I Love Him, I Love Him for He Is Mine; Isn't the Love of Jesus Something Wonderful.

Preparation
If you want the young people to read the verses, write them on slips of paper and give them out in advance. They are: I John 4:9; I John 4:10; Rom. 5:7, 8; I Cor. 6:19, 20; Heb. 3:15; Ps. 16:11; Song of Sol. 6:3; Prov. 3:12; John 16:23; John 16:25; Ps. 46:10; Phil. 4:13; John 17:10, 22; James 1:12; I Thess. 4:17.

Presentation
Valentine's Day is a day meant for sweethearts. It is thought to have first started at a Roman festival called Lupercalia. Then a Roman gentleman would pin on his sleeve the name of the girl who was to be his partner for the day. Later this day was used to honor St. Valentine but some of the customs of the Roman festival remained. It became an important time for young people who were thinking of marriage. In the 1600s

a hopeful young lady would, at bedtime, eat a hard-boiled egg and pin five bay leaves to her pillow, believing that this would make her dream of her future husband.

It is thought that the first valentine card was sent by the Duke of Orleans when he was imprisoned in the Tower of London in 1415. He sent love poems to his wife in France. During the seventeenth and eighteenth centuries sweethearts exchanged handmade valentines with yards of real lace.

Today valentines are much simpler and children trade them with their friends. There are still many valentines given between sweethearts, married and unmarried, and loving thoughts to members of the family and friends.

There is One, though, who has been sending us His words of love long before valentines were even heard of. (Hold up the Bible valentine.)

Today I have some valentines with a word or two written on them which were taken from the little candy hearts. They are meant to convey a message from one person to another. But I want to show you that God has the same message for us in His "Love Book," the Bible.

1. The first is *MY LOVE,* found in I John 4:9. (Hold up each heart and read each verse as you come to it.) Just before that in the eighth verse it says, "God is love." His love isn't just so many words, though; it is proven in actions. As verse nine said, He loved us so much that He sent His Son so that we who believe on Him might have eternal life.

2. And this is *TRUE LOVE:* I John 4:10. (Read the Living Bible version: "In this act we see what real love is: it is not our love for God, but his love for us when he sent his Son to satisfy God's anger against our sins.")

Many years ago the king of Abyssinia took a British subject prisoner and carried him to a dungeon made in the middle of a mountain. He was held without cause and the British demanded that he be released. The king refused. Soon 10,000 British soldiers were on their way to rescue the prisoner. The soldiers had to march 700 miles under burning sun and through mountains to get to him. After a battle at the dungeon, the prisoner was rescued and carried to a ship which quickly took him home to England. It had cost the British government $25,000,000 to rescue that one man.

It cost God even more to release us from the sin that binds us and keeps us a prisoner living an unhappy sinful life. It cost Him the life of His only Son.

3. Our next valentine should express our feeling when we read Romans 5:7, 8. (Read it before you show the heart.) *WOW!* Jesus Christ died for us while we were still His enemies. Can you imagine anyone having love like that?

4. There are two sets of words on this valentine, *MY GIRL,* and *MY BOY.* Let's read I Corinthians 6:19, 20. Christ bought us with his blood. Now we belong to Him, if we accept His sacrifice and believe on Him. Isn't it great to belong to One who loves us so very much?

5. And in love God says, *SAY YES.* The verse is Hebrews 3:15. As God said to the children of Israel, so He says to us: "Don't harden your heart when you hear My voice."

6. God says, "I want you to be *HAPPY.*" Psalm 16:11 says it.

7. We will be happy too if we've formed this *LOVE KNOT.* In the Song of Solomon we find a verse which speaks of the relationship of the Christian, called the church, and God. Read Song of Solomon 6:3. Such closeness we have with God.

8. Sometimes, though, God has to tell us *NO,* don't do that. Read Proverbs 3:12. He loves us too much to allow us to go the wrong way and get hurt.

9. Christ's love and His Father's love is shown in another way too. They love to give us the things we need and the things we would like, if they are in His will. So Jesus said, *"ASK DAD,"* or Father. Read about it in John 16:23.

10. Jesus also says, *"ASK ME,"* in John 16:24. Isn't it wonderful to have Someone who wants to show His love to us in a practical way?

11. Of course there is a time to quit asking and God says, *"KEEP STILL."* That's in Psalm 46:10. Yes, there is a time just to be still. Perhaps our asking has come to the begging, selfish stage. It isn't, "Lord, You give me what You know is

best for me," but rather a demand: "Give me." Or perhaps God wants us to wait a little while as He says in Psalm 37:7, "Rest in the Lord, and wait patiently for him."

12. Do you think that is hard to do? Well, our Heavenly Father says, "You *SURE CAN*." Paul believed it too as it is recorded in Philippians 4:13. With a loving God at our side "all things are possible to him that believeth" (Mark 9:23b).

13. Did you know that this spiritual family is *TRUE BLUE?* We're connected to a royal family. In many places the New Testament speaks of the Kingdom of God. Jesus came to this earth "preaching the gospel of the kingdom of God" (Mark 1:14). So if there is a kingdom, there is also a King, and we who are in the spiritual family are children of the King. Yes, we're all together in this royal family. Read John 17:10, 22.

14. All in all, it's a *BIG DEAL*. A little of this "deal" is found in James 1:12. Not only do we belong to the royal family, but we can also expect the crown of life.

15. And some day Jesus is going to say, *"LET'S FLY."* Read I Thessalonians 4:17. And with all these promises, we should bring out again the valentine that says, *"WOW!"*

16. I've shown you God's Valentines, but now here is mine; *WILL YOU?* Will you be God's valentine? Will you give Him your heart, a heart full of love? He offers His heart full of love to us. How much is that love?

One mother asked her little girl how much she loved her. The little girl thought awhile as she looked out the window. Then gazing up at the star-filled sky she replied, "All the way to the stars and back again."

That is how much God loves us, all the way from heaven and back again. He has demonstrated that when He sent His Son. The Son is now preparing a place for those that love Him. Accept His love and give Him yours in return. You'll find how wonderful He is and will be able to repeat this poem which is adapted from a valentine.

> More and more I realize
> With every year we share,

The wonderful Savior I accepted
Is the dearest anywhere.
And the love that's in this Valentine
Is meant for Him alone,
The Savior I'm so proud of
And so glad to call my own!

23

Sweet Repose

Object
A sleeping bag

Purpose
To help young people to trust in God and let Him solve their problems.

Suggested Songs
Safe Am I; Teenager; Only Believe; I Believe God; I Just Keep Trusting the Lord.

Preparation
Before the service ask some young fellow to be prepared to come and lie on the sleeping bag when called.

Presentation
Today I want to talk about something which is suggested by a sleeping bag. The word is *rest*. I'm not going to suggest you get in earlier from your dates and get more sleep. Neither am I going to suggest that you not work so hard on your studies; although there might be times when both bits of advice could or should be wisely followed. And please don't get so relaxed as we talk about resting that you fall asleep.

Will [some young man] come up and *rest* on this sleeping bag? (Have him lie down and completely relax.) Now he is doing what Webster says: he's in a state of ease; there is an absence of motion; and he's pausing from any labor or exertion. He's also enjoying (?) repose, at least I think he is.

That looks like one of the simplest things anyone can do but there are times when resting is the hardest thing to do. We may look like we're resting but we really aren't, for our minds are going eighty miles an hour. And that is breaking the speed limit. We can't seem to turn off our thinking apparatus; we tend to thrash over all the thrills and disappointments of the past and make great plans for the future. Too often we spend this time in worrying. This lack of rest is harmful to our body and mind. Jesus knew this for He told His disciples to "Come ye yourselves apart into a desert place, and rest a while" (Mark 6:31).

Jesus was much more concerned about spiritual rest. He talked about resting in Matthew 11:28-30. (Read.) The twenty-eighth verse suggests heavy burdens on our weary backs. What are some of these burdens? The first and greatest is *sin*. It is a burden because of guilt, the feeling that says, "Man, you shouldn't have done that!" The other burden of sin is the impossibility of not being able to stop doing such things as lying, cheating, becoming angry, thinking dirty thoughts. But Christ Jesus offers rest from those burdens. As we come to Him, He takes them all away.

There are other burdens, though, and they come to us even though we are children of God. They're worrisome things such as sickness, poverty, temptations, persecutions, or just the inability to have what we want the most. This doesn't come only to adults. There are many children and young people with stomach ulcers, stomach pains, headaches, and nervous disorders which have come from worry or the failure to relax. True, we worry about different things. For the young person, it hardly ever is the worry of not having enough to eat, at least in this country. It may be rather the lack of money to dress like you wish, or "Where will I find a Christian boyfriend, or girlfriend or the mate God has for me?" There are numerous things teen-agers are uptight about today: inability to get along with parents and brothers and sisters, school work which is defeating them, lack of friends, self-consciousness, lack of spending money, or the unrest in the world in general which will get worse as the coming of Jesus draws closer. But through it all, Christ is saying: Come to Me and rest.

In India loads are carried on men's backs and heads. There are stones about three or four feet high set up along the roads. A man walking down the road with his load may back up to one of these stones, sit down, and rest his load on the stone.

An Indian Christian was praising the Lord one day and said, "Oh, that is what Christ is, my rest-stone." In a sense that is true, but He is even more than that. Christ doesn't just take the burden for a time but, if it is the burden of sin, removes it. If He doesn't remove our other burdens, He helps us carry them, making them bearable.

Of course, there is a part for us to play in all this. Matthew 11:29 speaks of joining ourselves to Christ with a yoke. That sounds like work, doesn't it? In a way it is, but it is an easy job. We're told that the yokes which were used for oxen were not always the same weight on both sides. Many times the yokes were fixed so that the weaker animal would not have to pull as heavy a load as the stronger one. That is the way it is with Christ; He takes the heavier part and leaves the lighter load for us.

There are too many times when we try to carry or pull the load by ourselves. Instead of resting in the Lord after we have done everything He has wanted us to do, we fret and worry and go through all kinds of motions that get us nowhere, except perhaps into trouble. David said, "Rest in the Lord; wait patiently for Him to act" (Ps. 37:7a, Living Bible).

Now let's go back to rest as Webster defines it. It is an absence of motion, a pause, peacefulness, quietness, and stillness. That is just exactly what resting in Christ Jesus is: we quit struggling and in peacefulness and quietness we say, "I'm going to stop worrying and trying to work this out myself. I'll just go ahead and do my best and live the Christian life as You want me to and leave the rest to You." Many times the Israelites tried to work out some of their problems with other nations in their own way. Often they got into a terrible mess. But God told them, "In quietness and confidence is your strength" (Isa. 30:15, Living Bible). As the nonswimmer is saved from drowning by stopping his struggles and merely resting in the hands of the rescuer, so we must rest and let God take over. He may tell us to wait for the thing we want or He may tell us what to do. It's our part to rest in Him, listen to His voice, and then act.

24

A Bottle of Medicine

Object
A bottle of medicine

Purpose
To emphasize the importance of a smile.

Suggested Songs
Let the Beauty of Jesus Be Seen in Me; Lord, Lay Some Soul Upon My Heart; Happy, Happy, Happy; You Can Smile.

Preparation
Bring a bottle of medicine. Make very sure that no one takes it.

Presentation
How many of you have dreamed about being a doctor? There is something about the profession with its art of healing that tends to put a doctor on a pedestal.

Today I have news for you. I can show you how to give out a remedy which acts like a medicine. You do not need a license to practice medicine. You cannot buy the remedy at a drug store. You cannot get it in a bottle. This medicine is found in Proverbs 17:22. (Read, in both the King James Version and in the Living Bible.)

Let's take a close look at this verse. (As you talk, show the medicine you've brought.) First, notice that the verse doesn't say that a merry heart is as costly as medicine. And it doesn't say that it tastes like medicine. No, it says a merry heart *does good* like a medicine. Let's make some comparisons:

1. Medicine makes a person feel happier, even before it has a chance to work. Just the idea that help is on the way perks *up* a person. And a happier feeling will show on a person's face.

A cheerful, happy heart will make you a happy person and happiness will show on your face. You'll be happy even when things aren't going right: you're faced with a tough algebra test, or your car broke down—again. You will have an inward trust in God and know that you have His help.

2. Medicine, as it goes to work, joins forces with our body and helps to heal us.

The last part of Proverbs 17:22 says, "A broken spirit makes one sick." It's a known fact that unhappiness and discouragement cause a great percentage of illness. Such things as high blood pressure, headaches, and stomach ulcers, can come from an unhappy attitude and worry. As we begin to take a positive, happy attitude, healing begins.

Unhappiness makes us ill both physically and spiritually. A worried or complaining spirit is not trusting God. That's actually saying, "God either doesn't love me, or else He's so weak that He can't help me." That, of course, is a sin.

3. Medicine gives the user a hope of a future life of health and happiness.

A merry, cheerful heart also gives us hope in the natural and spiritual life. We don't have a pessimistic outlook: "I'll probably flunk algebra," or "I'll never have any friends." Instead we are optimistic, looking for the good things in life. We know we are children of God and our future is in His hands, His very capable and loving hands.

A cheerful heart doesn't help only us but it helps those about us, too. A smile makes the other person feel better, too. They think, "Oh, good, someone likes me." Everyone needs friends, everyone needs to feel wanted. Proverbs has more to say about that. Proverbs 16:24: "Kind words are like honey—enjoyable and healthful" (Living Bible). Proverbs 15:4: "Gentle words cause life and health" (Living Bible). Knowing that someone thinks he is worthy of at least a smile makes others feel better physically and mentally.

How can this medicine of cheer help others in a spiritual way? Let's answer that with another question. To whom do you go when you have a problem? You go to someone who is your friend, someone you can trust, someone who will listen with a sympathetic ear. As you show a constant friendly attitude, giving a cheerful hello and a smile, others will think of you as a friendly person. Then when they come to you with their problems, you will have the privilege of pointing them to the One who has all power and all love, One who will be glad to help them as they surrender their lives to Him. Christ will then have the opportunity to heal them physically and spiritually. And it all started with a smile.

This whole thing has a way of snowballing. If someone finds a medicine that will heal the pain in his Adam's apple, he quickly runs to tell his friend who has a similar pain. And he in turn tells someone else. Soon many people are using Carter's Adam's Apple Cure-all.

Snowballing may well happen as you apply the medicine of cheerfulness. As you become known as a person who has a serene trust in God, others will come to you. And the one who has been helped will now be in the position to help others. There is no end to the possibilities that may result from just a cheerful heart. If you don't have a cheerful heart, go to the One who is the source of all happiness, the Lord Jesus Christ. Ask Him to come and live by His Spirit in your life. The more you get to know Him, the better you will love and serve Him, and the happier you will be. Happiness will be reflected in your face and you will be doing good, like medicine.